19629

D0450076

CHINA JOURNAL

by Emmett Dedmon

photographs by the author and Charles Bennett

RAND M^cNALLY & COMPANY

Chicago   New York   San Francisco

For Jonathan, like his father, a traveler

Quotations from Edgar Snow's *The Long Revolution,* copyright 1972 by Random
House, Inc., reprinted courtesy of Random House, Inc.; from John King Fairbank's
The United States and China, copyright 1971 by the President and Fellows of
Harvard College, courtesy of Harvard University Press

Library of Congress Cataloging in Publication Data
Dedmon, Emmett.
  China journal.

  Bibliography: p.
  1. China—Description and travel—1949-
I. Title.
DS711.D37   915.1'04'5   73-12850
ISBN 0-528-81821-X

Printed in the United States of America
by Rand McNally & Company
First Printing, 1973

Contents

Preface

China is a land and a nation waiting to be known. Like a young lover with ancient artfulness, she turns her face shyly to the world. After 24 years behind doors locked from both the inside and the outside, she now peers uncertainly at new guests, new friends, and new neighbors. A smile flickers about her lips as she speaks, but her eyes are guarded, cautiously assaying this new attention.

To know China today, you must feel and sense this mood. It is a new mood, for China and for the world—most particularly for the United States.

This journal is a personal report of this mood as the author found it expressed in personal contacts with the Chinese people in a myriad of settings during a 4,000-mile journey through an old land with a new face.

It is a journey that few Americans have been privileged to make or probably will be permitted to make in person for some time to come. It is a journey full of surprises. It is a journey full of change.

This journal is an invitation for you to make that journey with me, to make your own discoveries and to form your own opinions. In short, it is an invitation to share an adventure in travel among a people whose culture has always been one of the most fascinating fabrics in the tapestry of history.

EMMETT DEDMON

埃米特 代德门

Railroad tracks run under the covered bridge at the Hong Kong-China border, but everyone must walk. Baggage is transferred on handcarts.

1

Into the New China

You cannot ride into the People's Republic of China. You must get off the train that brought you from Hong Kong and walk.

The walk is a short one, up to a one-story customs-and-immigration building manned by Hong Kong Chinese in immaculately pressed British white linen shorts. Once past the immigration center, you walk across a railroad bridge, with a wooden floor and arched corrugated iron roof, to a border checkpoint at Shumchun, where Chinese soldiers in green cotton uniforms wait to collect your passport.

There are no barricades and no barbed wire. The space on the other side of the border is sunny and open. At one side is a large open-air waiting room where Chinese nationals are processed; beyond lies a large two-story building reminiscent of American railway stations of the 1920s, with large waiting rooms for processing groups of foreign visitors.

Tea is served almost immediately, as it was to be served almost inevitably throughout our stay. About the only instruction we have received is "Wait"; and so we wait beneath a wall-sized mural of Mao Tse-tung holding a half-smoked cigarette and painted Goliath-sized against a backdrop of China's mountains. The only other diversions are a series of magazines and Mao's Little Red Books in five different languages on bookracks along the wall.

Customs formalities are brief, but authorities require a detailed listing of radios, watches, jewelry, tape recorders, and other items that could be substituted for legal tender in a consumer-goods-hungry society. After customs comes money changing into yuan and chiaos (Chinese dollars and 10¢ pieces), and then to another room

Huge wall-sized mural of Mao Tse-tung greets visitors in waiting room at Shumchun. Note the cigarette—no cancer scare for 79-year-old Mao.

Chinese and foreigners surrender travel papers to soldier at other end of bridge at Shumchun.

for more tea—served under the pounding themes of propaganda music issuing from a loudspeaker at the corner of the room.

Always, even with the bright sunlight coming through the old-fashioned lace curtains, there is a sense of dealing with the unknown. We have no itinerary; we have no plan for the day; but after four years of petitioning, we are at last inside the real China, a country encompassing almost one-quarter of all the people who live on this earth.

No one can approach China without a sense of awe as well as wonder and curiosity. How can the mind, for example, grasp the concept of 800 million people? Or a land whose civilization goes back 5,000 years or more?

We visitors, a small group from the American Society of Newspaper Editors, are from a country where change is constant and where we have yet to celebrate our second century of nationhood. What will we find in a land that for several millenniums had been ruled by tradition?

How much freedom will the Communists give us? What about pictures? Or our tape recorders? Will we be free to ask the questions all Americans are asking about this country so long closed to Western eyes?

Our questions are to be answered, but not quickly. We seem to be in China, and yet not to be quite there. When officials do appear, it is merely to tell us what to do *now;* never are we told what we will be doing *next.* This feeling of being suspended in space and time between the Free World and the Communist World is emphasized as we are moved from one room to the other, always with exquisite courtesy—always with more tea—and always without word of the next move.

Will we be in Canton tonight? Will we be in Peking in time for the celebration of National Day the next day? No answer. But wouldn't we like to partake of some dinner while waiting for the train?

A train seems to be waiting outside the station. Is it our train? Then it starts to pull out of the station, and we are afraid we have lost a precious half a day. "No," says the guide, "it is not our train. There will be another."

He then leads us into a large dining room, and we settle ourselves at several round tables set for eight and await our first Chinese meal. It is the first of many surprising experiences.

Our noonday lunch, which for the Chinese is their principal meal, consists of chicken soup with egg noodles, a bowl of rice, spicy deep-fried sausage balls, boiled small shrimp with a sweet sauce, large deep-fried prawns in batter, cold chicken slices, hot boiled-pork fragments, and cold sweet-and-sour pork. There are various side dishes and spices, among which are the 1,000-year-old eggs, actually a kind of pickled egg in which the egg white has been converted to gelatin.

"We are actually getting very efficient," our young escort, Soong Wen-hua of the China Travel Service at Canton, tells us. "Now we can make 1,000-year-old eggs in three months!"

All of this is topped off with various kinds of sugar cookies and slices of moon cake, along with the bottomless cup of green tea. At lunch we have our first taste of "Pijou," the Chinese beer, a mild and refreshing alternate to the favorite soft drink of the Chinese, which is a kind of orange soda pop.

After the meal, we encounter the Chinese custom of "taking a little rest." In Latin America we would call it a siesta. Later in the trip, as the October days remained unseasonably warm, we realized that most of China is in the latitude of our southern states and for most of the year much of it has a semitropical climate, making the "little rest" a sensible escape from the heat of the day.

After our rest, accomplished in overstuffed chairs covered with beige cotton slipcovers, we are alerted that the train is in the station, that we are on our way to Canton, and that we will transfer directly to the airport there so we will be in Peking that night.

The effect of this announcement brings a group of editors, somnolent from overeating, out of their chairs to hurriedly collect their hand baggage. Outside, we find a train that, by contrast to the old wooden coaches which had brought us from Hong Kong to the border, is sleek and modern. Inside, we settle in a comfortable day coach with leather-covered seats. As the train pulls out of the station, a discreet cheer goes up from our group. The trip to China has at last begun.

As we looked out the window, we saw large green rice paddies as large as midwestern wheat fields, surely an unusual sight to anyone who has seen the tiny paddies of Japan, Thailand, or the Philippines. Two of our group, who had been in China with American military forces immediately after World War II, remarked how different it looked and commented on the immaculate cleanliness of the interior of the train, so untypical of the China they remembered. At short intervals, an attendant with a mop worked his way up and down the aisles, keeping the floor as spotless as it had been before the car was occupied.

Shortly a female attendant appeared with a tray of large tea mugs, each with its individual lid. One for each of us, along with a small bag of tea leaves, was placed on a small table by the window. In a few minutes, she appeared again with an ordinary aluminum tea-kettle, signaled for us to put the tea leaves in the bottom of the cup, and after asking if we wanted *cha,* poured the hot water directly into the cup. Thus Chinese tea—green, with no cream or sugar, but refreshing, surprisingly mild, and easily absorbed in large quantities without the aftereffects of coffee.

Inside the train, as we sped along over a flawlessly smooth road-bed, were some very comfortable Americans. Outside the windows was the new China—Communist China, mainland China, more formally the People's Republic of China—established on October 1, 1949.

When we reached Canton, we were whisked past a line of waiting journalists and officials to a motorcade of small cars that drove us briskly to the airport without even a nod at the stoplights we passed. But at almost every stoplight (there were not many), a policeman changed the signals to suit our convenience.

At the airport, we were greeted by Yu Chung-ching, of the Information Department of the Foreign Ministry, who was to be our escort throughout the tour. Quickly he rattled off information on press cards, telephone calls, filing stories, baggage tags, and a series of instructions that sent us scurrying to our typewriters to fill out forms, assuring us not only that we were in China, but that we were there officially.

The heat at the airport was severe, even in late September, and the Russian Ilyushin-18 turboprop, four-engine plane, sitting in lonely splendor on the ramp, had been in the sun for several hours. Boarding it, we were not surprised to find that it was hot; what did surprise us was the form of air-conditioning provided—wicker fans that the hostess took from the overhead rack and passed out to the passengers.

The plane was crowded; in fact it was sold out, and the distance between the seats was not designed for long-legged Americans. But as the Chinese were very casual about allowing us to put heavy hand luggage in the overhead racks, we were not as crowded as in the tourist section of a small American jet.

Although we were invited as guests of Hsinhua, the official government news agency, we had insisted on paying our own way. The Chinese agreed only reluctantly, but once they agreed they carried out our intentions to the letter; we were all charged for overweight baggage on the flight.

We arrived in Peking in the dark, and as we left the plane, were officially greeted at the bottom of the stairs with warm and friendly handshakes. Then we were driven past seemingly endless rows of multiple trees along seemingly endless and deserted boulevards until we arrived at the Peking Hotel, headquarters for the highest-ranking delegations invited by the government.

From our hotel window, we could look out to Tung Chang An Boulevard and beyond it to Tien An Men (Gate of Heavenly Peace) Square, where it had all begun for today's China.

How had this country come to be what it is today? And what had brought us here on this journey?

We had read thousands of pages to prepare ourselves for this trip, and I (alone among the group) had spent many arduous early morning hours mastering 1,200 Chinese characters so that I would have some language facility. After these preparations, we had come intending to make comparisons, but we soon learned there is very little in other nations with which China can be compared.

Today, China is not only like no other society in the world, it is not even comparable to other Communist societies. And to see China clearly, it is really necessary to glance back briefly.

Here, in Tien An Men Square, on October 1, 1949, Mao Tse-tung, heavily bundled up against the north wind, proclaimed the founding of the People's Republic of China. As awesome in size and design as Moscow's Red Square, this huge plaza in Peking lies immediately in front of the onetime Forbidden City, where past emperors, empresses, and their retinues and Pekingese dogs lived in royal isolation from the people.

Today the Forbidden City is called the Palace Museum, and it is open to every citizen of the People's Republic. The square in front, designed when the Chinese Communists were heavily under Russian influence, is now the symbolic center of Chinese Communism.

Large portraits of Marx, Engels, Lenin, and Stalin are mounted on massive slabs at one side of the square, while the benign countenance of Chairman Mao looks down from the entry gate of the onetime residence of royalty, with slogans of proletarian triumph on either side of him.

Mao had built his armies and the strength of his revolution on the support of the peasants in the countryside, and it was to the countryside that he turned first in trying to achieve his goals: to advance China "from an agricultural to an industrial country, from a new democratic to a socialist society and Communist society, and to abolish classes and to achieve world communism."

None of these loftily worded goals have been achieved a quarter of a century later. But what has been achieved is most visible in agriculture, and it was here that Mao placed his first emphasis.

His first objective was land reform, which he accomplished by ousting the landlords and forming the peasants into mutual-aid teams that pooled their efforts and their crude farm implements. Later the peasants joined cooperatives, whose land, livestock, and farm implements were centrally owned. As a final step, the government in the late 1950s implemented a plan of Communes, subdivided into Production Brigades and Production Teams, which permitted farmers to work together to apply mass-production methods to agriculture, even when it was necessary to substitute backbreaking labor for farm machinery.

Others have reported on the agonizing efforts that were necessary to make this transition. But it would be getting ahead of my story to tell how the experiment has finally evolved. Suffice it to say, we did not expect what we saw, and we did not see exactly what we expected.

Much of what has been achieved in China and much of what is in process of developing today has been accomplished through concentrated campaigns directed by the central government—which means by Mao himself.

Mao is one of those great figures of history who with their multiplicity of talents have changed the world—whether for good or ill. He is a poet, a leader of armies, a political genius, and a philosopher. For versatility of talent, perhaps he belongs in the exclusive company of Caesar, Napoleon, Jefferson, and Churchill—men of differing moral standards, but all men whose genius for government was only one aspect of their intellectual spectrums.

To talk of China's governmental structure is really to talk of Mao's moods. China's governmental lines of command are so amorphous today as to make Britain's famed unwritten Constitution seem a model of orderliness. Though Mao, in his conflicts with the Soviet Union, claims to be the guardian of pure Communist doctrine, he really has made Communism a servant of the nation's needs rather than the opposite, as Communist literature might want us to believe.

For example, when Mao wanted to eradicate the filthy conditions of the cities, with the disease and flies they attracted, he did it by mounting a huge propaganda campaign that engaged the whole populace. The results were successful, and he repeated the technique in dealing with venereal disease and dope. Every Chinese citizen was responsible not only for his own behavior, but for his neighbor's; if this impinged upon freedom or privacy, it was not Mao's concern.

Similar campaigns were mounted in the early 1950s. First came the "Three Anti" movement, directed against officialdom in the government, in state industries, and in the Party. The movement was anticorruption, antiwaste, and antibureaucracy—really an attempt to break the stranglehold that government bureaucrats had had over the life of the Chinese for thousands of years. It was not successful, but Mao would try again in 1966, and that time he would win.

Then came the "Five Anti" movement, which mobilized public opinion against all business that still remained in private hands. It was during this period, according to China expert John King Fairbank, that the encouragement of informers and testimony of neighbor against neighbor and class against class probably reached its zenith. By 1956 we are told, all private business had ceased to exist, and the bourgeois class as such had been eliminated. Everybody now worked for the state.

This campaign successfully concluded, Mao was ready in 1958 with another one, which he called the "Great Leap Forward." Its specific goals were to make the most effective use of rural labor by: (1) using unskilled rural labor intensively for irrigation, flood-control, and land-reclamation works; (2) raising agricultural productivity by using more hands to plant, weed, and cultivate the same field; and (3) expanding small-scale industry locally in order to produce equipment and consumer goods for the farmers.

The Great Leap Forward was a disaster in some respects. The economy was so disrupted that Mao was almost brought down from his place of power. By the early 1960s, however, the country was functioning close to normal again as the new irrigation projects, one of the goals of the Great Leap Forward, produced unexpected bonuses for agriculture.

Then in 1966, Mao launched his largest campaign of all, the "Great Proletarian Cultural Revolution." And that "revolution"— which took place just seven years ago—changed China as much as anything the Communists had done previously. (We had heard of the Red Guards and their part in the Cultural Revolution, but we were unprepared for the extent of the change that resulted. China had become a uniquely different kind of country with a different kind of government.)

Mao conducted the Cultural Revolution as he had conducted his earlier campaigns—by going directly to the people rather than operating through any governmental structure. In fact, he initiated the Cultural Revolution because he thought the governmental and Party structure was closing in around him, reducing his options, and ultimately intending to reduce his power. Faced with the choice of giving up power or smashing the structure, he chose to smash the structure.

In the fall of 1966, with the support of the People's Liberation Army (PLA), which he could still control, Mao transported throngs of young Red Guards (it has been estimated there were millions of them) to Peking. Here they were indoctrinated to the point of fanaticism before being unleashed upon a surprised Communist Party bureaucracy and government.

Through a series of marches, physical attacks upon "enemies of the masses," and "big-character" billboard denunciations of public officials, these radicals among radicals—actually mobs in the streets —disrupted all of China. Their goals, as given by Mao, were to destroy the "Four Olds"—ideology, thought, habit, and custom.

Their first targets were the educated upper classes and the intellectuals. So effective were their tactics that all higher education in China was brought to a complete standstill. The anti-intellectualism also extended to government officials and administrators of every kind of institution, a class the Chinese refer to as cadres. Finally, the attack switched to the Party itself, with Mao urging the masses to seize power as the Paris Commune had done in 1871.

With no built-in control and no positive program to substitute for what had been destroyed, chaos had to result. Finally, Mao had to call on the army to restore administrative order. To restore administrative continuity, he devised the Revolutionary Committee as the basic governing unit of the country and its industries and agricultural enterprises.

These Revolutionary Committees are the operating government of China today. They are based on the "Three-in-One" principle (another Mao slogan) of embracing the masses (workers), peasants (farmers), and soldiers at all governmental levels, as well as the old, the middle-aged, and the young (another "Three-in-One").

The administrators who had been replaced were expected to go to the countryside and to identify themselves with the peasant-soldier revolutionaries by engaging in work in the fields. Edgar Snow described it graphically as a demand by Mao that every generation should relive the revolutionary life experience of the original Communists (and, therefore, presumably reach the same conclusions). A comparable situation in the United States would be if we asked every generation to relive the early hardships of the pioneers.

On May 7, 1968, Mao issued a new declaration that refined this process by setting up May 7 schools, where people would not only do manual labor, but get highly organized political indoctrination at the same time. In the beginning, these schools were rather like reform schools for persons errant in their political thinking. By the time we arrived, however, the May 7 schools had changed substantially in tone if not in content and had actually become something of a status symbol.

These, then, are some of the modern forces at work in ancient China. To discover what they had changed and what had not yielded to change would be the goal of our exploration.

In one day, we had come from Hong Kong, one of the most international cities in the world, to Peking, one of the most isolated for a quarter of a century. But would we be allowed to pursue the puzzle?

That was the unanswered question as we went to sleep on our first night in Peking.

2

A Day in Peking

Translated from the Chinese, Peking means "northern capital." And the wind from the mountains of North China blows chill and hard through the streets of Peking.

There is an austerity about Peking that is a direct reflection of this severity of nature and climate. Endless miles of brick or clay walls stand faceless to the street, while the houses of Peking nestle protectively against their inner walls or are clustered in huddles around tiny courtyards, as if everything had been constructed with its back to the wind.

It is a wind to be fearful of, for bronchitis is a classic disease of Peking, aggravated in the cold months by the soft coal and charcoal used by most of Peking's 7,570,000 residents in their open-fire cooking and heating. The wind is not only bitingly cold, but the smog that forms in the air bites the nose and throat of the unwary stranger.

Our first morning in Peking dawned cold and gray. As I looked out the window of my room on the sixth floor of the Peking Hotel, the rooftops of the palaces of the Forbidden City floated like waterborne pagodas in the morning mist. Although it was only October, the air had the penetrating chill of a winter morning.

From the other side of the hotel came the toot of an occasional truck or bus; except for these noises, the city seemed still to be asleep.

The silence was deceptive. As I stepped past the soldier in his green tunic, who stood politely beneath the red banners and massive portico of our hotel, I found myself gazing over a gray-blue-brown river, flowing endlessly and silently down Tung Chang An

Bicycles dominate traffic on long boulevard leading to Peking's
Tien An Men Square. Houses are built against wall as
protection from wind.

Boulevard that led to Tien An Men Square. These were the people of Peking on their way to work, pedaling steadily, incessantly, and noiselessly on over a hundred thousand bicycles, in a stream that seemingly had no ending and no beginning.

The bicycle is the private automobile of China. It is expensive (for an ordinary worker, almost two months' wages), and along with a watch, a sewing machine, or a radio, occupies the same status among personal possessions as the automobile in America.

Chou En-lai was to tell us there were 1,700,000 bicycles registered to the 7½ million residents of Peking. In the morning and again in the evening, it seemed as if all of them were being pedaled past our hotel—every one at exactly the same speed.

As the bicyclists glided by, the drab colors of their cotton Mao jackets and trousers, which are the standard costume of Communist China, blended imperceptibly with the gray smog of the early dawn. The pace of the cyclists was eerily constant, as if their motion were controlled by some unseen mechanism, rather than by a myriad number of legs—all pedaling different machines, yet all moving at the same pace.

I did not realize it at the time, but this was a portent and a fore-shadowing of one of the mysteries of China today—the unseen force that controls the motion, the pace, and the goals of 800 million individuals and blends them into a pattern.

Occasionally the symmetry of the street scene would be broken by one of the double-hinged, two-coach electric trolleybuses pulling to and from the curb. But the only private cars to be seen were the rows of sedans and limousines parked in front of the hotel for trans-porting official visiting delegations such as ours.

We had arrived in Peking on the eve of National Day (October 1), the anniversary of the establishment of the People's Republic of China and a festive weekend comparable to our Fourth of July. Most of the people were required to work only half a day on Saturday, and in the afternoon, they poured into the streets to shop, to stroll, or to visit as Americans might on any similar holiday.

Wang Fu Ching, one of the principal shopping streets in Peking, was only two blocks from our hotel. Without interference from our guides or our hosts, I was soon part of the holiday crowd in the streets, walking with them, looking in the same store windows, and tasting the thin ice-cream wafers for sale at the portable tables and stands on the sidewalk.

We were, of course, not part of the crowd, but apart from the crowd. Our color was different, our size was different (most of us were taller than the Chinese), and our clothing was different; and the shiny chrome and black of the cameras that hung from our necks were duplicated only in the windows of the camera stores.

We were dressed in wool sport coats or sweaters. The Chinese were dressed in cotton Mao blouses and trousers, from some of which could be seen the edges of long underwear that had been donned as protection against the Peking wind.

Some of us had brought topcoats or raincoats as protection against the chill. While we might don a sweater or overcoat on the outside to keep warm, the Chinese method of keeping warm was just the opposite. The Chinese almost universally wear only the cotton Mao jacket and trousers as outer garments, but one did not need a laser beam to detect that there were layers of clothes beneath the rumpled cotton surface—the number of layers a secret known only to the wearer. Later, we deduced that the long sleeves on the Mao jackets, turned up in warm weather, were probably a practical concession to be turned down over the hands in cold weather to prevent the wind from whistling up the wearer's sleeves.

It was not hard to judge the mood of the crowd. They looked at us with curiosity but no real special interest. Later we learned that the political indoctrination courses to which all Chinese are subjected had been preparing them for the new sight of "distinguished foreign visitors" (from whatever country). As a result, the adults passed us by pretty much as they did their fellow countrymen, but the teen-agers could not contain their curiosity or surprise; I saw one chubby young girl give her two companions a discreet nudge of the elbow and an eye-signal in my direction, as if something really strange had suddenly appeared. I couldn't resist a *Knee how* ("Hello, how are you?") and was gratified with an outburst of teen-age giggles as the three girls scurried off down the street.

The holiday crowds jamming the double-hinged, two-coach electric trolleybuses were another measure of the mood of the crowd. People were not only jammed into the aisles; they were crushed into a single, shapeless mass, and under the sheer force of internal pressure, elbows, necks, and heads protruded from the windows in illogical sequence. So that the doors of the bus could close, the people still on the street shoved on the backs of those fortunate enough to get a foot in the door. Still, there seemed to be no ill-temper, and the whole boarding process was accomplished with hardly a word being spoken, as if it were a system learned by rote.

At the intersection was a food store comparable in size and merchandise to a medium-sized delicatessen in an American city, and one of the few lines we saw in China had formed outside. The reason was not a shortage of food or fresh vegetables, but the need

Bicycle parking lot and street crowds in heart of
Peking's shopping district.

Department store window in
Peking shows plain quality
of clothing on display.

to present ration coupons for the grain products on sale. At another grocer's a few doors down the street, there were no lines, and we could see plenty of fresh vegetables inside, as well as a bounty of sausages and smoked meats hanging in the windows, much as they did in a general store in the rural United States.

A clothing store displayed bolts of boldly colored material in the window, but we could see no evidence that any of it had been converted into dresses or blouses for women. Men and women dressed very much alike, the difference being the high collars on the men's costumes and the flat blouselike collars on those worn by the women. The only real color was in the clothing of the children, whom the parents were emboldened to dress as gaily as they might in any country of the West.

Sweaters in bright yellows and reds were also on display, and we saw colorful sweaters peeking out from beneath some of the women's jackets, while a few teen-agers wore jackets of plaid (much the same plaid was to reappear everywhere we went, by the way).

Next was a camera store, where cameras patterned after the Japanese models were on sale, as well as Chinese color and black-and-white film. We also found some black-and-white British film. Since developing Chinese color film might be a problem after we left China, we realized that the film we had was the film we would finish the trip with, so we prudently started to budget each day's supply.

In a country where no jewelry is worn (traditionally a wedding ring is never used), it was not too surprising to find that a watch-and-clock store was exactly that and no more. The styles were conventional, and neither this store nor the others we saw later were very crowded, indicating that though watches and clocks are within the means of most Chinese workers, they are still regarded as a luxury item. It was with pride that peasants were to tell us that every member of the family had his or her own watch.

Another shop featured bicycles and electrical products, such as light bulbs and radios, as well as a shelf full of replacement parts for bicycles. Nearby, a candy shop selling wrapped sugar candies was doing a flourishing business.

In a square set back from the street stood Peking's State Store, a three-story department store festooned with banners proclaiming the unity of the proletariat of the world and the anniversary of the People's Republic.

Because it was a holiday, there did not seem to be room enough in all the doorways combined to accommodate the people entering and leaving. But somehow, in the polite Chinese way, all of us managed to slither by each other and into the interior of the store.

Inside, displayed in conventional glass counters was a variety of practical merchandise. Packaged colorfully, if not very stylistically, all of it was geared to practical personal needs. There were no real surprises, although an American shopper might find the lack of escalators or elevators a hardship; the only way to the third floor was up three flights of concrete stairs (which were constantly being swept clean of candy wrappers and cigarette butts).

As foreigners, we were able to buy cotton products without ration coupons, and we emerged equipped with a Mao cap (20¢) and a cotton Mao jacket ($8). One interesting feature of the store was a tailor's counter on the third floor, where tailors were busy cutting and rough-stitching material that had been purchased in bolt form by the customers. One could only be awed by their speed.

At another counter, some light gray Mao jackets must have been on sale; a line had formed around the counter, and the clerks were hastily fitting one customer after another, while seemingly comparable Mao jackets at a nearby counter received hardly any notice. How did the Chinese know they were on sale? Our Chinese hosts simply said they knew. Another Chinese mystery.

Returning to the street, it seemed that the stores we had seen earlier were reproducing themselves. An exception was two bookstores, one for Chinese-language books and the other for foreign-language books. In the latter was a large room where the only products were the books, the poems, the pictures, the personal souvenirs related to Mao Tse-tung, available in more languages than I cared to count.

In a smaller room nearby was a variety of English-language books on China, as well as a supply of Chinese-English dictionaries and basic grammars and readers for learning Chinese. I made a few purchases of these, for I had already found that the romanization (transliterating the Chinese ideographs into the alphabet) that I had been using for my 1,200 words of Chinese was not the system used in Peking. I had decided that, if my Chinese were to be useful in the future, I would have to be able to read it in the modern style the government is attempting to standardize throughout all China.

Foreigners have one shopping advantage not available to the Chinese—the Friendship Stores in all major tourist centers (though until tourists are freely admitted, the phrase "tourist centers" may be an anachronism). These Friendship Stores offer a variety of Chinese handicraft items, jewelry, ivory carvings, and linens for export. Unlike stores for foreigners in other countries, the Friendship Stores list all their prices in Chinese currency; foreign currency is not accepted. But a small branch of the Bank of China down the street quickly makes the necessary supply of 10-yuan notes available to the buyer.

The 10-yuan notes are interesting, for they are the largest denomination of money available in a country where the average wage is less than 100 yuan per month. Thus the American tourist with the desire for a piece of jade costing several hundred dollars will find himself with a rather thick fistful of money as he returns from the bank to the Friendship Store to claim his purchase.

After I had made my rather modest purchase of an antique one-piece jade bracelet, the clerk reached into the plain, green metal cabinet behind him and brought out two jade rings—one cost 75,000 yuan (about $35,000), and the other, 60,000 yuan. Anyone who bought either one would have needed a porter to carry the 10-yuan notes back to the store.

In Peking, there are actually three Friendship Stores, all located within the same block. The first features the jewelry and handicrafts of contemporary China. The second has a limited number of antiques—some of which are brocades that have been converted to table throws from draperies and gowns once worn in the Imperial Court. These are very inexpensive, bear the red-wax seal, or "chop" that certifies them as genuine antiques, and until the supply is exhausted, must rate as one of the best buys in China. The third Friendship Store is a small version of a department store and offers mostly practical items for sale.

No one should expect to find precious antiques or art objects of exceptional value for sale today. Export of anything over 80 years old is forbidden, except with the government red-wax seal of permission. This seal is not given to valuable art objects or to anything made of rosewood, a Chinese specialty for centuries.

Returning to the Peking Hotel from our shopping excursion, we found individually addressed invitations in our rooms, inviting us to a state banquet that night in the Great Hall of the People. Our hosts were the Foreign Ministry; the guests were principally members of the diplomatic corps in Peking and leading government figures.

The banquet was called for 7:00 p.m., and we were told by our Chinese escorts that we must be prompt and that while the Chinese do not wear ties, it would be appropriate for the American guests to wear coats and ties.

We left our hotel by car, and when we arrived at the floodlighted area of Tien An Men Square, it was filled with lines of automobiles, more automobiles in fact than we were to see at one time in all of China. The cars were parked in a series of lanes in the plaza under police direction, the passengers scurrying up the broad monumental steps of the Great Hall like so many ants on an anthill. Across the street, thousands of Chinese watched silently and in perfect order without a police line or barricade in sight.

As we entered the great entry hall, it was as if a Grand March had been announced; every guest seemed to have arrived at the same time—as in fact they had. There were 1,500 of us, walking together into the ballroom, sitting down at designated tables, all within a space of about five minutes. Then, without ceremony or announcement, the head table filled up equally as quickly.

Presiding at the head table was the foreign minister, Chi Peng-fei. Chou En-lai was there. So was Mao's wife, Chiang-ching. At Chou's right was Prince Sihanouk of Cambodia, a reminder to the Americans present that not all our problems in Southeast Asia are within the boundaries of the Vietnams. The vice-chairman, Tung Pi-wi, was there; the vice-premier, Yen Cheh-lon, and the vice-premier for economics, Li Hsien-nien. Some of these were officials we hoped to interview later. Fortunately, the Chinese did not let us waste our time in official interviews, but at the time we did not know that all of China spoke with but a single voice.

The promptness was not unique to this occasion. A Chinese dinner begins on time and ends without dawdling. We learned that a 7:00 p.m. invitation means exactly that; you are to arrive at 7 p.m. sharp, not earlier and not later. When we gave a dinner for our Chinese hosts and interpreters at the Peking Duck restaurant, our guides made sure we were there by 6:55 p.m. Then, at seven o'clock on the dot, about 60 Chinese walked through the doorway; coming from different parts of Peking in more than two-dozen cars, they had somehow managed to arrive as Chinese courtesy requires—exactly on time.

The state banquet was a Chinese feast. Arriving at our places, we found 13 dishes on the table in a variety of sculptured patterns and all covered by a sheet of thin plastic, which was removed by the waitress only when the master of ceremonies (every Chinese banquet has one) announced that the banquet had begun. When our wine was poured, Chou En-lai arose to give a two-minute toast to the Revolution, to his country, and to the friendship of all peoples. After his toast, we all rose and clinked our glasses with the others at the table, while at the long speaker's table, the 100 or more honored guests rose and walked from one end to the other in a circular single-file pattern, until everyone had touched the glass of everyone else at the table. The graciousness of this gesture, with its emphasis on personal contact, was to be experienced again and again;

at various banquets of 50 or more, our host would go from table to table until he had touched his glass with that of every American guest.

Our state banquet continued under the supervision of the most efficient corps of waitresses I have ever seen. The plates were changed frequently, and woe be to the guest who had not finished because the waitress removed the dishes as she arrived with new delicacies. Among these were five-fragrances duck, peacock-tail fish, deep-fried sausage, the everpresent bean curd, slices of moon cake, and chicken soup.

As we talked about future plans with our Chinese hosts over green tea and super-sweet sugar cookies, the master of ceremonies rose to the microphone again. "The banquet is ended," he announced. It was exactly 9:00 p.m.

We made our way out through the grand entry hall with 1,500 others, and somewhere in hundreds of cars of exactly the same model and color, we managed to find ours.

Back at the hotel, I was much too excited to sleep, and with John Sengstacke, the black publisher of the *Chicago Daily Defender*, I walked back to Tien An Men Square to take color pictures, some of which are reproduced in this book. We had no escort, and as we took our pictures, only curiosity was in the faces of those who surrounded us to watch John with his movie camera or to look in fascination at the collapsible Japanese tripod I was using to take the slow time exposures required for night photography.

We had been in China only 24 hours, but already I knew the shopping center almost as well as I know Chicago's State Street. We had been shopping and celebrating a holiday with the people of China, and we had joined their most powerful leaders at a state banquet. It would have been a full day even in New York or Los Angeles.

3

I Have Seen Acupuncture and It Works!

In the United States, it is unusual, if not almost impossible, for an ordinary person with no medical training to witness an operation. Before going to China, the only time I had been in an operating room was as a patient.

But on an early October morning in Peking, I found myself in a small waiting room near the surgical unit at Friendship Hospital, donning medical garb so that I could witness not one, but four operations—all to be performed under acupuncture anesthesia.

To tell the truth, my stomach was a bit queasy. I had never seen human flesh cut open with the firm slash of a surgeon's scalpel, and I thought to myself that Dr. Chang Wei-hsin, the personable medical director of the hospital, was carrying Chinese hospitality a bit far by proposing to initiate my nonmedical colleagues and me with a four-incision spectacular.

As we were dressing, the four patients who were to undergo the operations walked by in the hallway and nodded to us in greeting. There are those who believe that acupuncture anesthesia is really a form of hypnosis and that the patient is mentally conditioned to feel no pain. But all of us agreed that the four patients on the way to the operating room were both normal and casual in their responses.

As the patients did not seem surprised or frightened by the group of white-garbed foreigners around them, we asked Dr. Chang if they had been told that outsiders would be witnessing their operations. He told us that they had been informed; they had not been told that we were editors, only that we were "distinguished foreigners"—a recurring Chinese phrase—who were interested in

Chinese medicine. True enough, and the patients accepted our presence with no self-consciousness.

The four operating rooms were located around a central scrub room, where the doctors washed up and donned sterile clothing. With about ten American editors roving about the operating rooms with unsterile cameras, it was obvious to a visitor that the Chinese were much less strict about sterile conditions in the general area of the operation than Americans; but it should also be said that in the immediate area of the surgical table or the cart with the operating instruments and sterile cloths, they were just as fussy as their American counterparts.

When the patients were on the tables, Dr. Chang took us from room to room, explaining the procedures that were about to be performed. In the first room, a woman patient was to have her thyroid removed. In the next room was the most serious surgery—the removal of a tumorous uterus. Across the hall, a 17-year-old boy was having a hernia repaired, and in a smaller operating room nearby, the doctors were removing a cataract.

Acupuncture—both treatment and anesthesia—is based on an ancient Chinese theory that there is another force in the body besides the circulatory and nervous systems. The use of acupuncture to treat ailments goes back before the time of Christ, when Chinese records tell of its being administered with a piece of sharp stone called a *pien*. (Metallurgy was still unknown.)

Acupuncture theory postulates a system of 12 paired vessels carrying pneuma (their concept of a life force or spirit), blood, and the Yang and Yin principles of weakness and strength or of male and female. Ancient charts show the location of such imaginary vessels and the 365 points at which needles shall be inserted to cure disease or to relieve pain.

More recently, Dr. William Gutman of New York City, in a foreword to *The Chinese Art of Healing,* lists 690 acupuncture points on the skin, clustering along 14 lines, or meridians, which Chinese medicine recognizes as containing points where acupuncture is effective.

Acupuncture anesthesia is a very recent development and can truly be attributed to the development of Chinese medicine under Mao. The Chinese report that more than 400,000 patients have now undergone surgery with acupuncture as the anesthetic and that the rate of success (for the anesthetic effect) is about 90 percent.

The Chinese willingly admit that acupuncture anesthesia still has some imperfections. At some stages in certain kinds of operations, patients still feel pain, particularly when the visceral, or internal,

At Peking's Friendship Hospital, acupuncture needles are connected to electrical system by tiny red electrodes. Woman did not flinch when needles were inserted alongside her nose.

organs are manipulated. Doctors also report that occasionally some of the needles are withdrawn wholly or partially during the operation and then reinserted later to reduce postoperative pain. Through experience, the Chinese doctors are also learning to reduce the number of needles required; one publication reports that successful anesthetization using only one needle was achieved in more than 400 operations involving the opening of the chest area.

The acupuncture needles are surprisingly small (three to six inches). They were wheeled into the operating area on a small cart attached to an electrical system. While the doctors soaked their arms and gloves in a sterile solution at one side of the operating room, the nurses and technicians inserted the acupuncture needles for the anesthetic. The patients did not flinch (or bleed) during the placing of the needles, and later we were told that each had been given a mild sedative of 25 to 50 milligrams of Dilantin early in the morning. This sedative was given only to enable the patient to relax during the placing of the needles, which provided the real anesthesia. The importance of acupuncture anesthesia is that it eliminates much postoperative shock. It cannot, of course, be exported to the West until doctors are able not only to show that it works but to explain *why* it works. To this end, the Chinese are doing extensive and intensive research. But so far, a scientific explanation of *why* has eluded even acupuncture's most skilled practitioners.

The placing of the needles was different for each patient, being related to the area of the surgery. The needles on the boy undergoing the hernia operation, for example, were inserted mainly on the side and leg. The woman whose thyroid was being removed had needles only in the head and neck.

Once the needles were placed, a technician attached several of them to small red electrodes that provided periodic charges of electricity; in the case of the hernia patient, this caused his foot to jerk each time the electrical charge was received. As he was still wearing his brown cotton socks, it was a little eerie to see his foot keep moving as if it were receiving some independent instructions of its own.

The operating tables were set up much as they are in American hospitals, with high-intensity, circular lighting overhead. Large floor-to-ceiling windows provided maximum daylight, and each interior wall was covered with a snakelike series of pipes to provide heat in the wintertime.

There was no sign of the highly sophisticated equipment we associate with movies or TV reproductions of operating rooms in American hospitals. Suction at the operating table (to keep blood and

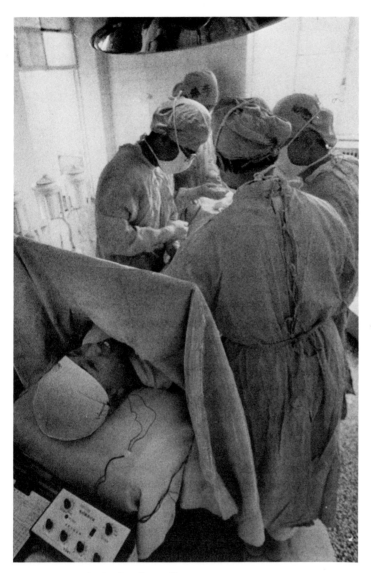

Woman is anesthetized with needle in ear.

loose pieces of flesh from the incision) was provided by a long red rubber hose, which looked as if it had been taken from a high-school chemistry lab. This hose ran to a big ten-gallon jar near the wall; the jar in turn was hooked up by a similar hose to a central suction pump.

With the first cut, we lost several of our colleagues, who decided to go back to the waiting room and drink tea. But after several tentative glances, I discovered that surgery—at least Chinese surgery —was a very neat process, and I peered into every incision and photographed it with the ardor of a newly ordained representative of the *Journal of the American Medical Association*.

As the operations were being performed, a nurse would occasionally give the patient tea by inserting the spout of a small teapot in the corner of the mouth. The whole atmosphere of the operating area was one of casual professionalism. When we asked about the amount of electricity in the current going to the acupuncture needles, the surgeon casually put down his scalpel, walked over to the electrical cart, and told us (through the interpreter) "six to nine volts."

With the aid of the interpreters, we were able to talk with all four patients throughout their operations. Even when we were not talking with them, we could see that they were conscious and not in great pain. One of these conversations led to one of the most revealing incidents of our trip.

We had heard so much about how the thoughts of Chairman Mao permeate the thinking of every Chinese that we asked the young hernia patient if he was thinking about the Chairman's thoughts while on the operating table.

"No," he replied casually, as we glanced down to a hole about four inches long that had been opened up in his side, "I was really just thinking about getting back to my job at the factory, because I feel no pain, and there is no need to think of other things."

"But if you had felt pain," persisted our chairman, Ed Murray, "did you have a saying of Chairman Mao ready to help you?" Murray, the president of the American Society of Newspaper Editors, was the spokesman for our group.

"Yes," the boy said, as if it were a natural thing to discuss Chairman Mao on the operating table, "then I would have thought of one of the Chairman's sayings—'we should be resolute, fear no sacrifice, overcome all difficulties to achieve victory.' "

In another room, the surgeons were sewing up the eye of the cataract patient with a small curved needle almost invisible to the naked eye (the cataract had been lifted by the application of dry ice). In the first operating room, the thyroid gland of the patient sat neatly on a table, the acupuncture needles had been removed, and the patient was being helped to sit up on the edge of the operating table. Supporting herself on the arm of a nurse, she slipped her feet into her sandals and started down the hall to her room. The doctors told us she would have some pain over the next 24 hours but otherwise no postoperative reactions. We had seen it all, from beginning to end, and there was no alternative but to believe what we had seen.

Although the operation for the removal of the uterus was still in progress by an all-woman team of surgeons, Dr. Chang invited us back to the conference room for a discussion of Chinese medicine and the delivery of medical care to the people of China.

There are two major hospitals accessible to visitors to Peking. One is the Capital Hospital, only a few blocks from the Peking Hotel and the major shopping center. It is an old building and was founded in 1905 by British and American missionaries as the Peking Union Medical College. It was taken over by the Rockefeller Foundation in 1915, and prior to the Liberation, many of the hospital's doctors were trained under exchange arrangements with Billings Hospital of the University of Chicago. During the Cultural Revolution, the name was changed to Anti-Imperialist Hospital, and the present name was adopted only on January 1, 1972, just before President Richard M. Nixon's visit.

(I was taken to the Capital Hospital when I developed a severe laryngeal infection, so I was pleased to learn that it was now flying a more neutral nameplate and that I would not be treated as an "imperialist." After an examination in a rather dim and dingy room by a woman doctor in a gray smock, a treatment of penicillin was prescribed. Although I told the nurse I had received penicillin in the United States and was not allergic to it, she would not give it to me until after I had passed the allergy test they administered. The penicillin itself was in the form of a series of eight capsules of fluid and eight of powder so that I could carry it with me—another example of their practical approach to medicine. Any nurse or "small doctor" (paramedic) could administer it wherever I might be traveling. And, as it is for the Chinese themselves, this medical care and medicine were free).

Friendship Hospital, where we witnessed the operations, was a so-called general hospital serving about a million people in the southeast sector of Peking.

Dr. Chang, the medical director, also carried the title of vice-chairman of the Revolutionary Committee. Between 1941 and 1946,

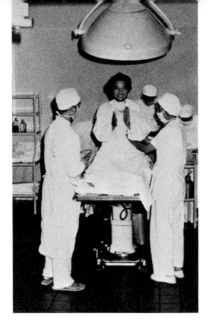

After removal of thyroid, woman sits up on operating table and responds to applause of visiting Americans who had watched the operation.

Young boy, still wearing socks in which he walked to operating room, patiently waits for hernia operation to begin. During operation under acupuncture anesthesia, he talked to us about the thoughts of Chairman Mao.

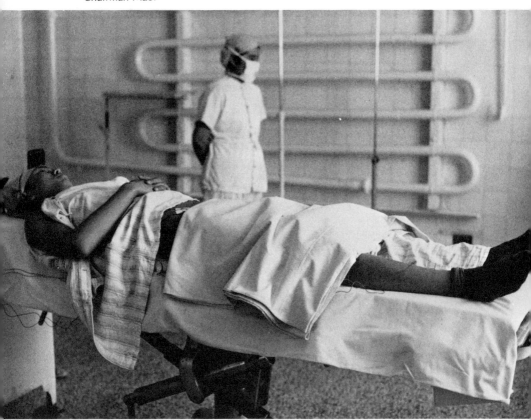

he had done pediatric work at Los Angeles County Hospital and at both Children's Hospital and Peter Bent Brigham Hospital in Boston. He was one of the most articulate men we met in all China, and the only official to carry on an interview with us in the English language. Dr. Chang had spent two years in the countryside, helping deliver medical care to rural areas, so he was able to give us a firsthand view of medical theory and practice as it has been structured since the Cultural Revolution. His return from the countryside was also an indication to us that the government had recognized it had pushed the glorification of manual labor too far and was beginning to recall many skilled people to their pre-Cultural Revolution posts of responsibility.

Was it really necessary, we asked, for a man of Dr. Chang's skills and qualifications to go down to the countryside? If so, we asked, what had he been doing wrong that made it necessary for him to spend so much time among rural peasants?

His answer was not obsequious, but it reflected the same vocabulary and tone that every Chinese seems to have learned by heart. He explained that in his view many doctors in the hospital had been "unconsciously following Liu Shao-chi's revisionist line prior to the Cultural Revolution. We looked on ourselves as specialists, as an elite class," Dr. Chang said.

When we asked how he could be sure they were not on the wrong track now, he replied evenly that it could be demonstrated through the intellectual change in the doctors and particularly in their relationships with nurses and patients. For example, there was no longer a specialized division of labor; each person did·what was needed to serve the patient—whether it meant allowing nurses to write orders if they had sufficient experience and skill to do so or the doctor's getting or emptying a bedpan for a patient if that happened to be required while the doctor was in the room. All intravenous feedings are initiated by the nurses (many hospitals in the United States require an intern or extern). The doctors might even mop the floor, if no one else was around to do the job!

Dr. Chang told us the hospital was built in 1952 and has 610 beds. The staff sees about 2,500 to 3,000 outpatients per day at the hospital and various clinics. Many of the patients in the hospital for treatment are referred to it from one of the 110 clinics and 7 satellite hospitals serving the same area.

There are 594 medical personnel at the hospital, of whom about 200 are doctors, an equal number are nurses, and 89 are technicians. More than half of the doctors are women, and all of the doctors in obstetrics-gynecology are women.

The staff sees the hospital as having three functions: treatment, teaching, and research. In treatment, they try to combine Western medicine with traditional Chinese medicine. Theoretically, a "first-grade" teaching medical professor receives the highest possible salary in China today—345 yuan per month ($148.35). The top practicing physicians and surgeons make about 255 yuan per month; staff physicians, about 70 yuan per month; beginning physicians, 56 yuan per month.

One of the doctors with whom we talked was Dr. Sun, the chief of surgery, whose salary is 155 yuan per month. His wife, a dentist, makes 135 yuan. This combined salary, equivalent to $125 per month in the United States, might shock an American doctor. But Dr. Sun told us they have three children in school, "a TV set, several radios, and consider ourselves as having quite a lot."

We were at first surprised by the candor with which the Chinese discussed their personal financial situation and budget. Later, we learned that all salaries are set after a discussion by the particular group in which one works, so there is very little reason to remain secretive about it.

Dr. Sun told us that food costs about 20 yuan per month per person, and rent and utilities each cost about 10 yuan for the family. He pooh-poohed a suggestion that there were very few recreational opportunities under the Communist regime and said that he was quite happy to spend one day a week with his family in the park or on a holiday. In fact, he said, he did not have time for the professional reading he would like to do.

Later, we learned that one of the reasons for this shortage of time is the heavy political input in the administration of the hospital. One afternoon per week is designated for political study (although this might also be a cover for discussions of preventive medicine or delivery of health care). Another afternoon is set aside for general rounds and hospital techniques, including something called "responsiveness to patients' needs." Usually one evening per week is for separate meetings of the 17 clinical departments.

As with other key personnel installed since the Cultural Revolution, the chairman of the Revolutionary Committee and therefore the top administrator, was an army man. The political orientation of the hospital was also evident in Dr. Chang's description of the medical teams that the hospital sponsors in line with Mao's admonition that the major emphasis in medical work should be in rural areas—the countryside.

These medical teams are usually manned by volunteers, who are allowed one visit per month to return to their families (a weekend plus travel time, it was explained). We were told that in 1970 alone, 140,000 doctors, nurses, technicians, and other medical personnel were transferred from the city to rural areas. Older doctors are usually given assignments on the plains, while the younger volunteers go to the mountainous areas. The members of these medical teams also do manual labor, which Dr. Chang told us in his case often meant shoveling the famous night soil, the manure that provides life-giving fertility to the soil of China.

One of the principal health problems faced by these teams was snail fever, caused by bacteria that mysteriously appear on the snails living in the night soil. The bacteria enter the human body from the back of the snail while the workers are in the flooded rice paddies. In severe cases, the disease causes the stomach to distend and interferes with the circulatory system. Health experts have made a rough guess that 10 percent of China's rural population has some form of the disease. However, there is also a widespread belief that the sanitation measures imposed by the Communists, plus plastic boots worn by the workers in the paddies, may have done much to cut this figure.

A typical medical team in the rural area consists of about 15 people and is a self-contained unit, usually with a surgeon, internist, and obstetrician, as well as nurses and laboratory technicians. Their orders, which have remained constant since they were originally formulated by a Communist Party Congress, are to: (1) serve workers, peasants, soldiers; (2) put emphasis on prevention of disease; (3) integrate traditional and Western medicine; (4) organize on a mass scale for preventive action.

The fourth mandate resulted in the organization of the Patriotic Health Movement, which, through propaganda, "big-character" billboards, and neighborhood action, was responsible for the fantastic cleanup in China and an end to most flies, dogs in the cities, and rubbish in the streets.

Augmenting the work of the traveling medical teams are the "barefoot doctors," so-called because in the south these part-time doctors often go barefoot. In the north they are called "small doctors" and wear shoes; it's too cold otherwise. These "small doctors" generally have about three to six months' training—usually during the winter when there is little work to be done in the fields. They are selected for this training by the agricultural teams of which they are a part, but the candidates must also show they can absorb the needed education. There are about three to five of these paramedical workers to each brigade of peasants (a brigade is usually about 1,000 people).

"Barefoot doctor" in Commune writes prescription for patient.
Despite primitive character of offices, the "barefoot doctor"
program is effective.

Basically, these part-time doctors are taught to treat common diseases, to lance an abscess, to check the patient's temperature and blood pressure, to treat an infection, to set broken bones, and also to recognize symptoms of serious illness, such as an abdominal obstruction. Doctors from the Commune hospitals supervise their work and make regular inspections. When not treating patients, these amateur doctors work in the fields alongside the patients they will be treating later. Dr. Chang told us it was customary to give these "barefoot doctors" the highest work-point rating (participation in the income of the Commune) regardless of whether they were out in the fields or in a clinic.

Two areas of particular attention in the past decade were venereal disease and drug addiction. The latter, we were reminded correctly, was forced upon the Chinese against their will during the Opium War, which began in 1839. Venereal disease was attacked by treating prostitution as an illness rather than a crime. Prostitutes were first "cured," then given training for a trade. Also, as China moved along its Maoist, puritanical way, the market for prostitution vanished.

Dr. Chang talked at length of what he called the new "moral tone" in China as being the key to the solution of both the VD and drug problems. "When young people have a goal," he said, "there is no point in taking drugs. When the emphasis in a young person's life is upon real-life objectives, he has no desire to seek escape." One may quarrel with some of China's methods in establishing these goals, but Dr. Chang's statement that "the root of the solution to the drug problem lies in the values of society and the prospects for youth in that society" gave us plenty to ponder. We wondered how this concept could be developed into a consensus in a free society such as the United States.

We also asked about abortion. Dr. Wang Tzu-wen, the head of obstetrics, said that education in planned parenthood was principally carried out through Street Committees. The principal contraceptive method used is the pill, usually dispensed through the clinics at the Communes, factories, or schools. Extramarital or premarital sex, they assured us, was extremely rare, as were pregnancies of single women.

Doctors perform about five to ten abortions per day and require that the abortion be performed in the first three months of pregnancy. If the abortion is within the first 40 to 50 days, it can be performed at a clinic, and the woman sent home; after that, she is required to enter the hospital. Dr. Wang estimated that 85 percent of the women in the district served by the hospital take the pill, of which there are two kinds, one that can be taken once per month and one that must be taken daily for 22 days.

Acupuncture is also used successfully in a relatively high proportion of cases for the treatment of deafness, with special schooling being provided to augment the treatment. There are special workshops for the deaf, the physically handicapped, and the blind. The Chinese do not have our concept of separate welfare payments; rather, the state guarantees that each person, whether injured on the job or physically disadvantaged, will receive enough income for subsistence. Each Commune, for example, must set aside a certain amount of its income for this purpose.

Another area of medicine in which the Chinese are acknowledged to be ahead of their Western counterparts is in the restoration of hands or feet severed from the body. We saw several patients who had had these restorations, though we lacked any technical knowledge that might have permitted us to evaluate what we saw.

Because of the improved overall delivery of health care, the Chinese are living longer. And with longer life come new diseases.

A decade ago, a Chinese hospital handled almost no cases of heart disease, hypertension, or cancer. That was when the life expectancy was about 50 (as nearly as one can estimate in this land of vague or nonexistent statistics). Now that the life-span has been extended into the middle 50s, these diseases occur as frequently as they do in this country (indicating a virus doesn't know the difference between a Communist and a capitalist). Another example is in the area of mental health. There is only one psychiatric facility in all of Peking and, the Chinese candidly told us, a real need for more. The Chinese medical teams visiting the United States are even now concentrating on treatment of these diseases and illnesses, as well as birth-control techniques and treatment of bronchitis, a severe form of which is among the few remaining plagues in Peking.

As we left the Friendship Hospital, after seeing that our four acupuncture patients had been safely returned to their rooms, we asked ourselves if we would be willing to trust ourselves to acupuncture anesthesia. I believe I can honestly say that for most of us the answer was "Yes."

4

Peking University–From Campus to Coal Mine

If there is any one thing China needs most today, it is scientists and specialists capable of dealing with modern technology. And this is exactly what China is least likely to get as a result of the application of the theories of the Cultural Revolution to higher education.

In China, a graduate of a middle school (high school) has almost no option of going directly on to the university, even if he may show the precocity of an Albert Einstein, a Thomas Edison, or an Enrico Fermi. First he must go to the rural areas or a factory for one or two years. Then he will be accepted at a university only after he has won the approval of his fellow workers to pursue his education.

We were told in Hong Kong that the "freedom swimmers," mostly young people who escape from China each year, have increased from 11,000 to 18,000 per year. After investigating the system for higher education, this is not too surprising; a young man who dreams of electronic circuitry can hardly be expected to keep that dream alive during two years of hauling night soil to the fields.

There is some evidence that Chairman Mao Tse-tung is aware that the principle of mandatory manual labor may have been carried to extremes in its application to the universities. We detected a tendency in conversation to blame these extremes on "the ultraleftists," who seem to be emerging as the villains in this society. Perhaps the way is being cleared to correct the excesses and mistakes of the Cultural Revolution, which are nowhere more evident and depressing than in the state of higher education.

We were fortunate to get a firsthand view of how these educational theories are applied when we visited Peking University, set in a large sprawling park on the outskirts of the city. There we were greeted by the vice-rector, Chou Pei-yuan, a professor of theoretical physics who had earned his doctorate at the University of Chicago in 1926 and later taught at the California Institute of Technology. He was vice-president of the university before the Cultural Revolution and is one of the few university administrators or faculty members to survive without a trip to a reeducation camp or a term in the countryside to achieve a greater identification with the masses. In the party with him to greet us were several professors, two students of journalism, and the administrator of the university, Li Chia-kuan.

The vice-rector told us that Peking University has a long identification with revolution. On May 4, 1919, the students at the university started an uprising that was crushed. Mao Tse-tung himself was at the university at various times between 1918 and 1921. In 1949, when Liberation occurred, the enrollment policy of the university changed, and there was the beginning of an effort to enroll students from among families of the peasant and worker classes.

When the Cultural Revolution occurred, Peking University was closed, although the students remained on the campus. For four years, there were no university activities in a formal sense. Then in September 1970, enrollment was resumed. When we were there, the university had a total enrollment of 4,300 versus a total before the Cultural Revolution of 8,000 to 10,000. The university was hoping that by the fall of 1974 the student body would be as large as it was prior to 1966.

The university was founded in 1898 and has 17 departments with 64 disciplines. There are 2,200 teachers for the 4,300 students, but only 700 of the faculty are engaged in teaching, another aftermath of the Cultural Revolution. The majority are working on textbooks and other materials so that higher education will all be properly oriented to the Mao point of view. In addition to the classrooms, the university operates ten small workshops, or factories, where the students put into practice what they have learned.

Later in the afternoon, we visited one of these small factories in a one-story, concrete-brick building where they were making pharmaceutical materials, among them insulin, vaccines, and blood coagulants. We were told that the machinery had been designed and installed by students in the engineering and biochemistry departments and was being operated under the direction of a 56-year-old woman factory manager. The conditions did not meet the antiseptic standards of American pharmaceutical houses, but the areas were rigidly clean, and the employees wore hair caps and white smocks. Outside, another group of students were at work; they were digging air-raid shelters, an indication of how pessimistic China is about the possibility of war with the Soviet Union.

Pagoda and smokestack are symbols of
Peking University, where "production" and manual labor
are intermingled with higher education.

The structure of the university reflects its heavy revolutionary orientation. The rector, or chief executive, is Wang Lien-lung, a cadre member of the People's Liberation Army. He serves as chairman of the Revolutionary Committee, which functions as the directing agency for the school. It would not be correct to call the committee a Board of Trustees because its members have direct operational responsibilities. This committee is made up of seven military personnel, six workers, six administrators (they call them cadres), nine teachers and other staff members, three campus employees, seven students, and one "family member," which the English-speaking faculty present translated as "housewife."

Much of the early orientation of the student fanatics and Red Guards who initiated the violent excesses of the Cultural Revolution was carried on at Peking University (called Peita). It was from Peking University that the first student groups swept out to smash the old bureaucracy. From the present concern with preparing new texts and a new curriculum, it is also clear that the university sees itself as the primary custodian of the doctrine of the new China.

Historically, the educated had always been a distinct elite in China, and the Cultural Revolution was directed in part against what was considered the separation of the intellectuals from the common man. In the current political rhetoric, it is referred to as "the revisionist line" of Liu Shao-chi, who was deposed as chief of state in October of 1968 and is presumably alive somewhere in China undergoing political reeducation in carefully guarded confinement.

The principle of putting intellectuals above the rest of society in China dates all the way back to Confucius, who considered scholarship the highest form of virtue. The scholars were also the core of the government bureaucracy, which actually controlled the country in the name of the emperor. These traditions, of course, caused the gap between the intellectuals and the peasants to be wider in China than in any other country and therefore more difficult to breach and heal.

According to Edgar Snow, one of the reasons Mao initiated the Cultural Revolution was a belief that bourgeois-trained directors of middle schools and universities were weeding out the peasant-born and worker-born students—those with an inferior start in life—by designing tougher and tougher examinations. Courses were gradually being lengthened instead of shortened. Education was lapsing back into harmony with the principles of Mencius, who said, "He who uses his mind rules; he who labors with his hands is ruled."

A few phrases in my notebook reflect the new and current Chinese view of education, which emerged after the Cultural Revolution.

The students had been "cut off from the masses" and from "practical experience." They did not look at learning from the "viewpoint of the needs of the proletariat" but from the point of view of "gaining their own fame and fortune." Their education didn't meet the needs of "socialist reconstruction."

This was the message that became increasingly clear when the vice-rector had finished describing the general nature and structure of the university and turned the forum over to the chief administrative officer, Li Chia-kuan.

Questioning brought out that Mr. Li had a surprising background for an educational administrator. He was formerly a middle-management executive in the headquarters responsible for industrial production (factories) in the Peking area. He had attended the University of Nanking, but as there have been no degrees granted since 1949, he obviously had no academic honorabilia. Originally, he had been a member of a propaganda team of soldiers and workers who had been sent to the campus of the university. He himself had been a propaganda lecturer before taking on his present assignment.

As might be expected, his approach to education was doctrinaire. He described the purpose of education as being to "unite, educate, and remold." He was very critical of the previous tradition, which he described as being the Liu Shao-chi line of concentrating on knowledge without practical experience, and said it resulted in merely the creation of an "intellectual elite." At another point in the discussion, he described the goals of the university as "teaching, research, and production." To achieve this, science students are sent to work in factories (chemistry students to synthetic plants, for example), and liberal arts students are sent "out into society itself."

One of the notable dissenters to this educational philosophy had been Lu Ping, the former president of the university. Former president Lu, we were told, was now engaged in manual labor on a Commune; his salary had been reduced from 345 yuan per month to 150 yuan per month, "enough to take care of him and his family," as the Chinese put it. The Chinese did not rule out the possibility that with sufficient "political reeducation," Lu Ping might come back to the university, but we were definitely told it would not be as president.

After discussing Lu Ping, the faculty members were asked what had happened to the professors who had been at the university before the Cultural Revolution. We were told that with one exception, besides Lu Ping, they were all still there. The faculty members were pressed pretty hard on this, and it developed that many of them, including the professors at our table, had, however, been sent to the countryside for reeducation. Then began a series of low-key personal narratives that could not quite be called confessions but were close to being so.

Wu Chu-tsun, a professor of English who had been a student at Columbia University from 1948 to 1950, told us that he had been on a May 7 school reeducation farm for two years and that these had been "the happiest years of my life." For ten months, he had worked in the fields and then had spent the balance of the time teaching English to farm workers. English is the big educational fad at the moment, dating back, even before Nixon's visit, to the break with the Soviet Union and the development of contacts with Canada and Great Britain. Now English is even more popular, and the radio is offering English-language classes for a half hour each day, at 12:30, 4:30, 6:30, and 9:30 p.m. Professor Wu told us that at first, because of his age, they wouldn't let him work in the fields, but he insisted and said, "At least let me stand in the rice fields." He went on to say that in his opinion "all intellectuals need reeducation because they were all guilty of bourgeois thinking and some of them, feudal thinking." All that professors thought about until the Cultural Revolution, he said, was a high salary, material comforts, and the freedom to carry on as they pleased. "We didn't know how to serve the people," he said. Such is the life of an intellectual in Chinese universities today.

Professor Chou Yi-liang, Harvard-educated from 1939 to 1946, with degrees in history and Sanskrit, told of spending a month in the coal mines with his students. He was asked what he did there. "Shovel coal," he replied.

It is extremely difficult to get a firm organizational plan of any program in China today, and this was also true at the university. "Everything is still in the stage of experimentation," we were told.

As near as we could ascertain, a student spends nine months of the year in school and three months on a work-experience program, of which one month is physical labor in the fields and two months are spent in what is continually translated as "investigations." The professor goes to the countryside with his students, so it is possible to continue the educational process. We also learned that the physical labor might be on the basis of one day per week over the three-month period, which would of course make it more palatable.

An example of these "investigations" was given by Professor Chou, who said his students had been interviewing workers in the coal mines about their experiences under the old regime and the ways in which the Liberation had changed their lives. These interviews would be the subject of term papers, and then the professor would integrate them into a new textbook he was preparing on the history of the Revolution.

In addition to classroom training, the students get regular political indoctrination from the soldier-worker propaganda teams (which also function at the factories and Communes). Two and one-half days per week or one hour per day every day are devoted to discussing the history of the Communist Party, world Communism, the history of the Chinese Revolution, politics, and economics.

Since the Cultural Revolution, all middle-school students wanting to go on to the university must first have qualified as peasants or workers and earned the approval of their co-workers in order to continue their education. A young Chinese boy or girl must first make application and then present this application to the other workers in his factory or rural Commune. If they approve, the application is forwarded to the local Revolutionary Committee, where additional approval is required. Once these ideological hurdles are passed, the would-be student must pass an examination administered by the university of his choice. Until recently, these entrance exams had been abolished as relics of the old regime, but admitting students with untested aptitudes created many problems, and entrance exams now have been reintroduced.

The state pays for tuition and room for students and allows them 19½ yuan per month for meals and pocket money, an adequate amount by Chinese price standards. If, however, a student has been a worker for as long as five years before entry into the university, the state continues his salary throughout his college career.

The elite character of scholarly life for the faculty persists, even though their life-style has been changed to include regular periods of manual labor and "going down to the masses." "First-grade" professors earn 345 yuan per month, the top-level salary in China. Beginning professors earn 56 yuan per month, the same as a beginning physician.

Later, we visited an English class taught by a Chinese version of Mr. Chips, a Yale graduate whose British intonation made even us a bit self-conscious. His students, most of them in their early 20s, paired off to do several exercises of English dialogue, and these were impressively well-done. When we asked the names of one pair, they were written on the blackboard as:

Chen Yu-hsin (soldier)
Hu Chuan-chun (worker)

The soldier-worker designation was obviously important in this Maoist structure, where every individual must be identified as making a contribution to society.

Though the English class was impressive, in general the atmosphere of the university—which the Chinese admitted was representative of higher education throughout China—was depressing.

The only theoretical research underway at the university was in the area of elementary particle physics (the specialty of Vice-Rector Chou) and in acupuncture anesthesia, a hallmark achievement of Communist China.

I came away from Peking University with the feeling that the faculty were trying, without too much success or grace, to adapt university-level education to Mao's personal educational philosophy as he had outlined it in July of 1968.

"It is still necessary to have universities," Mao said (grudgingly one suspects), but then he hastened to qualify this by adding, "Here I refer mainly to colleges of science and engineering. However, it is essential to shorten the length of schooling, revolutionize education, put proletarian politics in command, and take the road of the Shanghai machine tools plant in training technicians among the workers."

The Workers' University in Shanghai, to which Mao referred, is one of China's showplaces. Operated in conjunction with a machine tools plant, it now has an enrollment of almost 100 students drawn from more than 20 factories. Each student must have at least three years' experience as a worker.

The workers live in dormitories connected with the factory and get full pay and fringe benefits. The courses offered reflect Mao's vocational view of education; they include higher mathematics, hydraulics, English, mechanics, mechanical drawing, design of electrical machinery and grinding machines (lathes), plus the usual political thought.

A graduate with whom our group talked called himself a technician and said he was now able to design new machinery. How creative a designer he could be with this education is a question that was not answered for us in China.

The Great Wall at Pa-Ta-Ling.

Peking and Environs

Great Wall

Chü-yung Kuan
(Nan-k'ou Pass)

Ming Tombs

Shih-san-ling
Shui-k'u

Nan-k'ou-chen

Ch'ang-p'ing

Kao-li-ying

Peking/Sha-ho-chen

Yang-fang-chen

Pei Ho

Sha-ho-chen

Ta-yü Ho

Ch'ing-ho

Ch'ing Ho

Summer Palace

K'un-ming Hu

Hai-tien

Ch'eng-tzu

Kao-ching

Hsi-chiao

Peking
University

Men-t'ou-kou

Ta-yü

Yung-ting Ho Aqueduct

PEKING

Shih-ching-shan

Forbidden City
(Palace Museum)

Ku-ch'eng

Subway

Railroad station

Ya-men-k'ou

Lin-ts'un

Marco Polo
Bridge

Feng-t'ai

Ch'ang-hsin-tien

Wan-
p'ing

Yung-ting Ho

Nan-yüan

Nan-yüan
Airfield

Hang-shui-ho

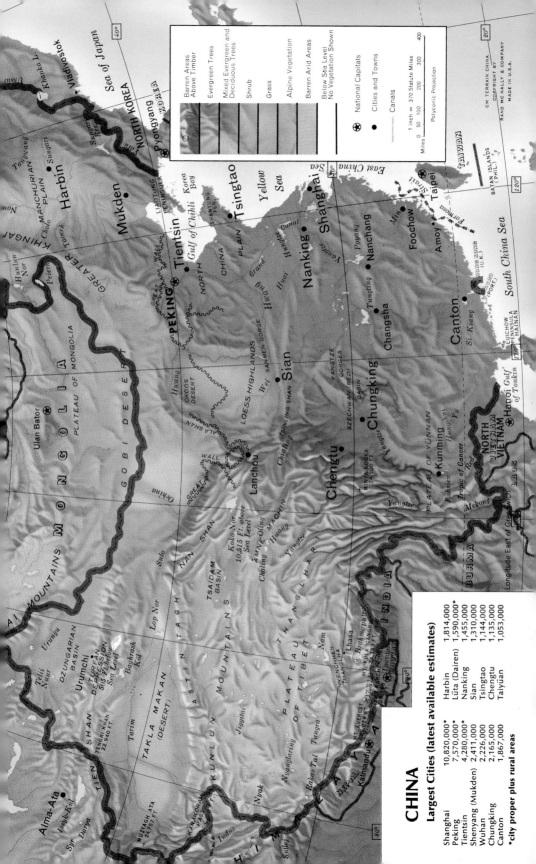

CHINA

Largest Cities (latest available estimates)

Shanghai	10,820,000*	Harbin	1,814,000
Peking	7,570,000*	Lüta (Dairen)	1,590,000*
Tientsin	4,280,000*	Nanking	1,455,000
Shenyang (Mukden)	2,411,000	Sian	1,310,000
Wuhan	2,226,000	Tsingtao	1,144,000
Chungking	2,165,000	Chengtu	1,135,000
Canton	1,867,000	Taiyüan	1,053,000

*city proper plus rural areas

Legend

- Barren Areas Above Timber
- Evergreen Trees
- Mixed Evergreen and Deciduous Trees
- Shrub
- Grass
- Alpine Vegetation
- Barren Arid Areas
- Below Sea Level No Vegetation Shown

⊛ National Capitals
● Cities and Towns
Canals

1 inch = 370 Statute Miles
Miles 50 100 200 300 400

Polyconic Projection

CM TERRAIN CHINA
COPYRIGHT BY
RAND McNALLY & COMPANY
MADE IN U.S.A.

Neat lines of beds and folded comforters at school and nursery of Textile Plant No. 4 in Sian.

Plump young boy on holiday reflects well-fed nature of children. Note his crocheted cap.

Young boy with toy rifle and bayonet affixed is trained
to think of himself as a future soldier or guerrilla fighter.

Nursery children at Ho Lan Production Brigade near Wu Xi
applaud the first Americans they have ever seen.

Schoolteachers
at May 7 school farm
near Peking do dance
called "Happy Are
the East Is Red May 7
School Freedom
Fighters Planting Rice."

Children celebrate National Day with pom-poms and dancing at the Summer Palace.

Children of Yenan display variety of colors and costumes as they applaud visitors and chant "Good-bye Uncle."

Young dancer at the Summer Palace strikes a pose for the camera during a rest period.

Classroom in day-care center of Tien Shan Workers Village in Shanghai.
In many places, students carry their own chairs to and from school.

Army couple poses proudly with their
daughter. Pockets at bottom of tunic
indicate they are both officers.

Teen-agers show an unusual combination of style
and color for a holiday at the Summer Palace.

Teen-agers march behind red banner on their way to countryside to help
with the harvest. They will live with peasant families.

Dancers' smiles come alive in setting of chrysanthemums and poinsettias, flowers that seem to be everywhere in China.

Folk dancers at the Summer Palace celebrate the glories of churning butter in setting designed for the Imperial Court.

Hall of Supreme Harmony dominates the courtyard of the
Forbidden City (now called the Palace Museum).

One of many throne rooms
in the Forbidden City. Note
sedan chair, in background,
which carried emperors.

Chinese on holiday crowd around souvenir
stand at the Summer Palace.

A night view of the Museum of the Chinese Revolution
and the Museum of Chinese History.

Schoolchildren pull primitive planter to sow wheat in dry clay soil. Later the field will be irrigated.

A member of the Shuang Wang Production Team harrows the soil in ancient manner.

A "labor hero" in Yenan who has twice been entertained by
Mao Tse-tung in Peking. Towel wrapped around his head is
traditional distinguishing mark of peasant.

Teahouse and willow trees form a harmonious
pattern at Huaching Hot Spring near Sian.

5

A "Friendly Conversation" with Chou En-lai

As the premier of China, Chou En-lai is the voice through which China speaks to the world. To meet him, to talk with him, to understand how he approaches international problems today, to get his thinking on the future of U.S.-Chinese relations—all of these were a primary objective of our trip.

We had been in Peking for a week without a response to our daily question: "Would we get to see Chou En-lai?" or "When can we see Chou En-lai?"

On Saturday, our moods shifted from depression to resentment as our schedule called for us to leave Peking the next day and there was still no interview scheduled with Chou. But at noon, we received an encouraging message.

"We hope our American friends will get some sleep this afternoon," we were told by Yu Chung-ching of the Foreign Ministry. "I also believe it would be advisable to have an early dinner and not leave the hotel without one of your Chinese hosts," he added.

Did this mean that we were to see Chou En-lai that night? we asked.

"I cannot tell you more," he said. This answer was echoed verbatim throughout the afternoon by the other interpreters.

We obviously had reason to hope that an evening interview was the reason for these instructions. They were easy for me to obey because having acquired a bad case of laryngitis from the Peking wind and smog, I left the hotel only to receive my penicillin shots at the Capital Hospital.

The evening seemed to drag interminably with no word of what might or might not be taking place. Then at 10:15 p.m., the interpreters and our hosts could be heard coming from their rooms down the hall and knocking on each of our doors. "In the lobby in five minutes," they said. "We are going to see the premier."

The interview, as is the case with most of Chou's official receptions, was in the Fukien Room of the Great Hall of the People. It was the same room in which he had held his private conversations with President Nixon.

Our late-night arrival was in considerable contrast to that of a week ago for the state banquet. Our two Red Flag limousines and ten Shanghai sedans were the only cars on the street, and we were driven right to the door on the upper arcade of the motor approach to the Great Hall.

We walked on broad maroon carpets through the great entryway hall to the Fukien Room, where Chou, his interpreter, and an official photographer awaited us. He greeted each of us individually in a ritual familiar to anyone who has ever had his or her picture taken in a receiving line with the President of the United States. Then he motioned for us to take our seats in the circle of old-fashioned overstuffed easy chairs near the center of the vast room. Between each pair of chairs were a microphone and a table for tea. At either side were several rows of conventional upright chairs for our Chinese escorts and members of Chou's staff and party.

The Fukien Room, where the previous evening Chou had entertained at a small dinner party for 12, could seat 700 to 1,000 people quite easily. The Chinese do not entertain for business or political reasons in their homes, nor is it customary for them to invite strangers into their homes. Thus, this huge hall—larger than the combined public rooms of the first floor of the White House—has become the locale for Chou's official entertaining.

Chou was clearly a man who is always at ease and accustomed to being in command. Skimming the list of Americans present, he inquired in Chinese (he speaks English well) as to which one of us was Charles Bennett, the managing editor of the *Oklahoma City Daily Oklahoman and Times,* whose pictures appear with mine in this book.

When Bennett identified himself, Chou recalled that Gen. Patrick Hurley, the ambassador sent by Franklin D. Roosevelt to China during World War II, was also from Oklahoma.

"I remember the first day I met him," Chou recalled. "General Hurley and I had just boarded the DC-3 airplane that had brought him, when he announced 'I'm a cowboy from Oklahoma' and let out a cowboy whoop."

Chou smiled as he recalled the scene (without reminding us that

Hurley was partially responsible for U.S. support going to Chiang Kai-shek's Nationalists rather than being used to force a reconciliation with the present Chinese leaders).

"Do you think you could give us an Oklahoma cowboy whoop?" he asked Bennett.

Bennett merely smiled and said he did not think he was the man for the job.

Chou seemed small in stature as he slouched between the broad armrests of his deep chair; but his head was that of a lion, with a high brow, bushy black eyebrows, and a mouth that seemed to lie across his face as if an artist had painted it with a single bold stroke of the brush.

Several of us noted that as Chou sat deep in his chair, he moved only his head and left hand. To drink tea, he would reach across his body with his left hand to pick up the cup. Later, during the break for tea, he explained that his right arm had been broken in a fall from a horse and had not been much use to him since. He did not smoke, a rarity among the Chinese in the room.

He spoke easily and with assurance, always taking the time to identify the editor who asked the question from the list in his hand. He remarked that one editor looked a little like Gen. George C. Marshall and another like Dr. Henry Kissinger.

When we commented on the hour of the interview and his heavy work schedule, Chou gave us this unusual self-portrait:

"In serving the people, I don't feel I have done well enough," he said. "You think I'm being modest, but I'm not. Everything I do is carrying out the decisions of the Party and the government. I'm only the executor, the implementer of the decisions.

"I don't get tired because I am optimistic. To do one's work well, one should be happy and optimistic . . . it is not good to be too tense.

"When one is very busy, it is easy to make mistakes. When mistakes are made, one should rectify them. When one is willing to rectify mistakes, then one can be happy and jolly (his interpreter's word). When one makes a mistake, one should be courageous and rectify it. Like when a person falls, he may bruise his leg but then he gets up and goes on."

His general comments had their point, of course. Chou had used the incident to set the tone of the evening. He wanted the conversation to be lighthearted and not deal with political polemics or substantive issues. Perhaps even the hour for the conversation had been chosen for the same purpose, for after he had given us the conventional greetings and expressions of friendship, he concluded

During interview, Chou En-lai toasts guests with cup of tea.

by saying he hoped this "would not be an interview" but a "friendly conversation."

Ed Murray, the spokesman for our group, replied somewhat tartly that we had had a "friendly conversation" with Chang Weu-chin, the deputy foreign minister, early in the week and that we really hadn't learned very much from it.

Chou brushed this comment aside. "Perhaps some others cannot answer because they are not sure what answers are permitted," he said, "whereas I can answer because I can make this judgment."

"Good," Murray replied. "Let's get down to some serious questions."

"Oh, why be serious," Chou quipped; but he settled back in his chair as the first fusillade of questions came at him from the circling encampment of editors trained in the art of the American press conference.

We were fortunate in being able to talk with the premier shortly after China had made two major foreign policy pronouncements, possibly the most significant restatement of China's goals and aims with respect to the outside world since the Bandung Conference of 1955.

The first statement was a major editorial in the *People's Daily,* the official national newspaper, on October 1, 1972. The second was a major speech by Huang Hua, ambassador to the United Nations, on October 3.

In the newspaper editorial, interspersed with long stereotyped repetitions of revolutionary vocabulary, was a reference to the fact that "even if a country previously adopted a policy hostile to China, we would hold talks with it for the improvement of relations between the two countries, when it indicates its readiness to change that policy."

The editorial also outlined the improved climate in international relations and credited Mao's five principles of peaceful coexistence as the basis for much of this improvement. These five principles are: (1) mutual respect for sovereignty and territorial integrity; (2) mutual nonaggression; (3) noninterference in each other's internal affairs; (4) equality and mutual benefit; and finally, (5) peaceful coexistence itself. The editorial also asserted that "the Third World is playing an increasingly important role in international affairs. Even some countries under fairly tight control of Soviet revisionism or U.S. imperialism are striving to free themselves from their dictate."

In his speech to the UN, Ambassador Huang continued this Third World theme. "A series of new victories have been achieved by the Asian, African, and Latin American peoples in their struggle to win and safeguard national independence. Countries of the Third World are getting united on a wider scale to oppose the superpower politics of aggression, expansion, and war," Huang asserted.

We asked Chou if these two statements taken together did not indicate that China was staking a claim to be the spokesman and leader of the Third World and if the recently published conciliatory statements about the United States and Japan did not indicate a softening of China's position as a leader in advocating world revolution.

Chou disposed of the second part of the question first by denying, with the firmness of an experienced doctrinaire revolutionary, that there had been any change in "line." "The foreign policy of China, as approved by Chairman Mao and the Central Committee, has followed the same revolutionary line for the past 23 years," he said.

Then, as he continued, his mood changed from one of animation to one of contemplation, and he seemed almost to be looking back in time. During those 23 years, he recalled, looking thoughtfully toward the high ceiling, it was "interference from within" as well as opposition from without that reduced the efficacy of China's foreign policy. He went on to make it plain that China's leadership had been badly split by the dispute between Mao and Lin Piao (former defense minister and Number 2 man in the hierarchy) and that, in his opinion, it had been only recently that even Mao had been able to speak to the world in a voice that represented a unified point of view within China.

On the issue of the Third World, Chou was vigorous and emphatic in denying that China would claim to speak for other nations or any bloc of nations. "We are not a superpower," he said, in a tone of voice that made it plain that "superpower" is almost as bad a term as "Soviet revisionism-imperialism" in the Chinese lexicon.

In another context, while commenting on the border dispute with the Soviet Union, Chou quoted Mao's dictum that an ideological dispute can go on for 10,000 years but that it should never be used as an excuse for a resort to force.

The "correct political line" in foreign affairs today, as reflected in the recent editorial and UN speech, Chou said, is that the superpowers should disarm and only then will world peace be possible. Meanwhile, China realistically accepts the fact that, despite its size, it is still very much a nation in a "state of development," a term Chou prefers to "undeveloped nation."

As an example of the identification of China's 800 million people with the smaller and middle-sized nations, Chou cited the surprising victory of the Albanian resolution in the UN on October 25, 1971, which admitted Communist China to the UN and simultaneously expelled Chiang Kai-shek's Nationalists. The necessary two-thirds vote was mustered from among the smaller nations.

Chou recalled that he had been with Kissinger in Peking when word reached them that the Albanian resolution had passed. The victory had surprised both Chou and Kissinger, who had expected the joint Japanese-U.S. resolution to carry—which to the Chinese would have been half a loaf and unacceptable.

Chou obviously admires Kissinger's skill as a negotiator and said that Henry could talk for a half hour without really revealing what he was thinking or giving out any information. Ed Murray told the premier that we had met some people in Peking like that too. Chou merely laughed.

Chou showed evident pride in the diplomatic niceties involved in both the U.S. and Japanese communiqués issued after the visits of President Nixon and Prime Minister Kakuei Tanaka, but he made distinctions in comparing the two documents. Since it was not possible to have diplomatic relations with the United States because of the Taiwan problem, the U.S. communiqué had to begin with a statement of major differences. "The first of its kind since World War II," he said admiringly. In the case of Japan, since it was possible to establish diplomatic relations, that communiqué emphasized the common ground of the two nations. But it should not be taken to mean they do not recognize they still have some major differences.

The discussion of U.S.-Chinese relations led quickly to the subject of Taiwan. Chou said that although he regarded Taiwan as a "fundamental problem" blocking formal diplomatic relations with the United States, Vietnam was the "more urgent problem."

He would not concede that there were any formal negotiations under way with Taiwan, but neither would he deny that there were contacts between the People's Republic of China and Taiwan. He even cited a recent discussion with a visitor from the island about the total governmental budget of Taiwan (more than $800 million)—which Chou said could be absorbed by the central government in Peking.

The moral of this last statement is plain; if governmental costs on Taiwan are taken over by China, the workers on Taiwan will find themselves in the pleasant situation (at least temporarily) of continuing at their old wages while being relieved of the income tax, which does not exist at the individual level in China. This is the message the Chinese are plainly trying to get across when they say the workers on Taiwan will be better off after a Communist take-over than they are at the present time.

Chou gave several examples of this soft-sell approach on Taiwan. As a precedent, he cited those areas of China where the Commu-nists were not in control in 1949 and where the conversion to Com-munist practices was gradual.

According to Chou, in some of the provinces, businesses and fac-tories were allowed to continue under their former owners and managers during the first seven years of the new regime. For the next ten years, they were paid a set rate of 5 percent per year on the value of their investment. Since 1966 (a date that coincides with the Cultural Revolution), everyone has been under the same pro-gram of wages and salaries prescribed by the state, though the former owners have been allowed to keep the income and assets previously accumulated.

Talking in part to American businessmen through his American audience, Chou told us that "even when these factories were short of raw materials while under private direction, we subsidized them by assuming the salaries of the workers during such periods of idle-ness."

One of the puzzles about which we wanted to talk to Chou was the question of the new leadership of China. Mao is 79; Chou him-self is 75. Where were the new leaders to come from? Who, of the younger men, could be counted among the leaders of China today? Another editor asked why it was that half of the positions on the Politburo, the ruling committee of the Party and therefore the coun-try, were unfilled.

It took Chou a long time to answer this question, even discount-ing the interruptions from his listeners. He would only deal with it in a historical context, and it was not too surprising that two of our group drew exactly opposite conclusions from his long discourse. One of them concluded that Chou was suggesting the Chinese would depend on collective leadership when Mao dies, much as the Russians did after the death of Joseph Stalin. Another made much of the fact that Chou for the first time had mentioned the name of Yao Wen-yuan, the radical young mayor of Shanghai. But my notes show that Chou had merely been responding to a question from this same editor, who had asked, "How about the young man from Shang-hai?" To which Chou replied, with a wave of his hand, "Oh, you mean Yao Wen-yuan. He is only one of many young leaders."

For myself, I drew no conclusions, for I felt he had only delin-eated the problem without giving any answer. What follows is a record of that conversation, and the reader may make his own evaluation of it.

It was true, Chou said, that the positions on the Politburo were only about half-filled. And he said, many of the members were old and infirm and did not attend the meetings.

With a touch of melancholia, he also referred to the fact that three of the members had died recently, two of them of cancer. He said that these deaths had been very much on his mind when President Nixon was in Peking and that he had therefore been extremely eager for a medical delegation from China to visit the United States.

But then as if to dismiss the subject, he said, "You seem very interested in the makeup of the Politburo. Is this because it is an election year in the United States?" To which he added, with a hearty laugh, "Anyway, your CIA branch in Hong Kong probably knows more about this subject than I do."

The statement was made without rancor, and it was apparent throughout the evening that the Chinese consider our intelligence apparatus, as far as China is concerned, the best in the world, with the Japanese a close second. The Russians, naturally, received poor marks from the premier. The British didn't get a mention.

Chou said the Russians' poor showing was surprising, particularly since they have the largest embassy in China and, he added slyly, the largest number of cars.

When we returned to the subject of leadership, he said those leading the state now are not few but many. And many are old leaders who go back to 51 years of struggle, 23 years since Liberation.

In 1921, he reminded us, the Party was young, inexperienced, and lacked mature leaders. (Only two founders of the Party, Chairman Mao and Marshal Chu Teh, are still alive. Chou signed on in 1922.)

Other leaders joined the Party in the 1927–37 period of civil war and land reform. These revolutionaries are now the most numerous among the leadership, and, Chou pointed out, most of these are over 60 years of age.

From 1937 to 1945, during the war against Japanese aggression, the armed forces grew to one million. This was the period, Chou recalled, when he had made the greatest number of friends from the United States. Those he mentioned were Edgar Snow, who had recently died; Owen Lattimore, who was visiting China at the time and who had had dinner with him the night before; Agnes Bentley; and Anna Louise Strong. He also was warm in his praise of Gen. Joseph Stilwell, who, he said, "had, with the support of FDR, been a source of great help to China."

The leaders from this period, he said, are now over 55.

Chou made particular mention of the "class of '38." In this year, apparently, the Communists experienced a huge surge in membership because of the Japanese atrocities. As he went around the room to some of the Chinese officials present, pointing them out, and saying "You were '38," I had the feeling that the "class of '38" is a group with a special esprit within the Party.

He reiterated what he had told President Nixon: The "old are too many and the young too few" in government. Then, pointing out that he had brought along some of the young for us to meet, he introduced a young man of 27; a young woman of 29; our tour escort, Yu Chung-ching, a 31-year-old employee of the Foreign Ministry's Information Department; and his boss, Ma Yu-chen, a suave 37-year-old senior official in the Information Department.

Unfortunately, Chou said, while those who are capable are many, those who are known are too few, and it is not possible to make them known quickly. "For example," he said, "because my name is too well-known, you would not have been happy if you had not had the chance to talk with me. That is why I knew that I should make room on my schedule to see you even though it was late on your last night in Peking."

Continuing with his long discourse on the history of the Party, he said that it had been made aware of the problem of "revisionism"— the danger of losing Communist momentum through dilution of ideology—by the difficulties of the Soviet Union, which began in 1956 under Nikita Khrushchev.

"Because China believes in ideological education rather than crude organizational methods, this was of critical importance to China," he said.

In 1962, a major effort was made to eliminate tendencies in organization that might lead to a return to capitalism. Then, in 1966, came the upheaval of the Cultural Revolution, during which the followers of Liu Shao-chi and Lin Piao, though few in number, had to be eliminated from positions of influence.

He was asked about the exact status of the former chief of state Liu Shao-chi, who is believed to be still alive. He did not reply directly but referred us to the case of Khrushchev, who, Chou said, had vanished totally. Then one day he suddenly appeared, and the press was full of him. Whether this might happen in the case of Liu, we could only speculate, but we had the feeling Chou was telling us that it might.

He denied a questioner's assertion that the Liu problem had shown the regime to be insecure. "There were very few followers of theirs," Chou replied, "and the facts have shown that all of China supported the moral tone of our leadership."

At midnight, attendants appeared behind our chairs, carrying plates of small cakes that we nibbled delicately so as not to miss the opportunity for a question. (The teacups had remained filled throughout the evening.) The questioning had been tough; without a doubt it had carried with it for Chou reminders of some of the major problems facing his country.

Suddenly, he stood up. "It is 12:20, gentlemen," he announced. "Let us take a break for tea and—to wash our hands." It was a welcome break, particularly as he indicated that it was not the conclusion of the interview and that we could resume our questioning after we had all returned to our chairs.

One of the questions we wanted to ask him was about the economic relations of China and the United States. Naturally, it came from Warren Phillips, editorial director and now president of the *Wall Street Journal*.

"Wall Street?" Chou chuckled. His answer underscored the fact that all decisions in China today, including economic ones, begin with political considerations.

"First we must determine the political line to be followed," Chou said, "and then apply it to other areas. Agriculture is to be the basis of our economy, to be followed in order by light and heavy industry."

He then gave us several examples of what he called the economic principle of "Walking on Two Legs." As an illustration of the principle, he cited a Commune near Shanghai where the wheat is planted in the same field before the cotton is harvested so that there will be three crops a year. "We must be self-sufficient in agriculture," he said. "It is inexcusable for a socialist regime not to have grain stored to guard against bad years."

He said this had been the worst year in nine years for Chinese agriculture because of the drought, but they had still been able to export rice and import wheat, thus securing a better balance in their grain supply. As the price of rice is sometimes as much as double that of wheat, this also helps the economy.

He did not believe Chinese agriculture would ever rely totally on chemical fertilizers but would continue to rely on night soil (manure).

As an example of the Chinese view that mechanization will not solve all problems, he said that even in the most advanced space capsules and computer systems, the most delicate parts of the mechanism must still be designed and made by hand.

He disagreed amiably with John King Fairbank's theory that the 1,700,000 bicycle riders in Peking would soon be adding motors to their bikes, then a third wheel, and finally they would be driving

At 2:00 A.M. Sunday morning, after innumerable questions,
Chou is still able to reply humorously.

autos. "In Peking," he said, "bicycles will always be bicycles, and cars will always be cars. If we convert them to cars, everything will come to a standstill, just like New York and Tokyo." He also indicated that pollution as well as congestion were reasons for rejecting auto transportation for commuters.

As another example of improving the balance of the economy— "Walking on Two Legs"—he cited a recent decision to emphasize the development of the interior and minimize the traditional emphasis on the coastal ports.

When asked about the possibilities of joint ventures with American companies, such as auto firms or manufacturers of agricultural implements, he said that this did not fit China's pattern today. He then went into a lengthy description of their joint venture with the Russians in mining and processing nonferrous metals.

"We didn't even need these metals," Chou said. "They had merely built a factory in China to serve their own needs. Then when Khrushchev got mad and tore up all his agreements, he took all his technicians home. We learned a lesson."

He also said Khrushchev had been quite serious in 1958 in proposing that the Soviet Union and China merge their navies into a single fleet. But Mao replied to Khrushchev that this raised only two possibilities: one, that you don't come at all or, two, that you take over and we go back to the mountains and guerrilla warfare. This was the beginning of the unhappiness that led to the withdrawal of the technicians, for whom, incidentally, Chou gave a dinner in the Great Hall on the eve of their return to the Soviet Union.

"Our industrial achievements since then may be small," Chou said, "but if it hadn't been for these incidents, we wouldn't be "Walking on Two Legs" as a nation today.

He said that even when China aids other nations, it does not propose joint management, though China would not oppose joint-venture agreements with other Third World countries that wished to enter into them.

The postmidnight conversation flowed on and on, as both the premier and those of us around him seemed to sense that there was so much to learn and so little time to explain. We subjected him to long interrogations about the fate of Liu Shao-chi, the former president now supposedly alive but imprisoned, and Lin Piao, former defense minister and once designated Number 2 man in the government, who was reported killed in an airplane crash.

It was 2:30 a.m. when the premier, still vigorous at 75, rose to walk with us out into the foyer of the Great Hall. By good fortune, my chair was near the door, and I found myself walking with him.

"How old are you?" he asked, as if the question of succession had not left his mind.

My Chinese was just good enough so that I could understand the question without translation and could answer him in Chinese.

"*Wu shih-ssu* (54)," I replied, hoping he would understand.

"You look ten years younger," he replied. Then he asked me how long I had studied Chinese. When I told him (in Chinese) 80 hours, he said, "Your accent is really not too bad."

Suddenly all those hours with my language cards and Catherine Chin, my Chinese teacher, had become worthwhile. And I was prompted to reply, "*Kwa tee-yang, Kwa tee-yang,*" which is loosely translated as "You flatter me." Whatever its idiomatic context, the premier and his interpreter both found it amusing; and so I was able to leave the premier of China laughing—at 2:30 a.m. on a Sunday morning.

6

I Go to the Countryside

It is a long way on the social scale from drinking Dragon Well tea with Premier Chou En-lai to sitting at table in the home of peasant farmer Li Hsin-chai at the Shuang Wang Commune, peeling a boiled yam. Yet the latter is exactly what I was doing on a sunny day in October.

We had been staying at nearby Sian, a textile center of 1,310,000 people, and a morning's drive had brought us to the Shuang Wang Commune, one of the showplace farms of the new China. On the way, we had passed through the county-seat town of Wei-Nan, where several thousand people had turned out to line the curbs and watch and applaud as our motorcade passed by.

Shuang Wang Commune itself is a revealing example of how Mao took the old village structure of China and adapted it to the communal goals of the new regime.

Shuang Wang was formerly the name of the village that stood at this site. In those days, we were told, it consisted of four rich peasant families and 42 poor peasant families. Nearby lived several landlords, who owned much of the land.

"Rich peasants? Poor peasants? Aren't all peasants poor?" we asked. "How could it be?"

The answers were a reminder of how little we know about how other people live and how deceptive language can be when we make the false assumption that the same words mean the same things to all peoples—or even mean the same in the East and the West.

In the years before 1949, or pre-Liberation as the Chinese say, there were actually five identifiable groups within what we would have merely referred to as peasants or farmers of varying degrees of prosperity. The factors that determined status were (1) the amount of land owned and (2) the percent of income derived from the land.

Because 80 percent of the Chinese people are engaged in agriculture and because it was upon these rural classes that Mao built his revolution, it is worth taking a look at the life-style they represented. Even today, just as Americans are likely to identify themselves as Hoosiers or Cornhuskers or Texans from the state of their birth, the citizens of Communist China still cling to identifications dating back to pre-Communist society. Thus it is that one person may say he is from "a small bourgeois family"; another will indicate he is from a "lower middle-class peasant family." (We noted that we met no one who said he was from a "rich peasant family.")

The rural classes, as explained to us by Yu Chung-ching, our slender and affable Foreign Ministry representative, were these: farmhand (short-term or long-term), poor peasant, lower-middle-class peasant, middle-class peasant, and rich peasant. The landlord obviously was not a peasant.

The farmhand, of course, owned no land. If he were a full-time farm worker (who, for instance, might be indentured to the landlord by his family), he was "long-term"; but if he were a poor peasant seeking to augment his income by extra work on someone else's land, he was "short-term."

The poor peasant usually owned some land, but so little and of such a quality that it provided only about 30 percent of what was required to sustain him and his family. Thus both he and his family had to work for others in order to make ends meet.

The middle-class peasant was considered to be self-sufficient, but with nothing to spare. The lower-middle-class peasant was probably not quite at that state. Both these groups, however, would suffer severely for food if there were a natural disaster, such as a drought, flood, or insect plague.

The rich peasant owned enough land so that he could not only sustain his family, but store some grain or sell it to provide additional comforts.

At Shuang Wang, the families who formerly lived in the village and others from nearby villages had now been gathered together into the Shuang Wang Production Team of 103 families, with a total population of 510 people. Of the villagers, 236 men and women were in the labor force, which farms about 100 acres of hard clay soil. Together they own 44 draft animals and 27 cows.

The use of more than 200 people to farm 100 acres seems strange to Americans; in the United States, the family farm is usually at least

90 or 180 acres. But in China, where machinery is scarce and even draft animals are rare, it is an example of how Mao has organized rural society in such an ingenious way that mass-production methods can be applied to agriculture by substituting highly organized and motivated hand labor for machinery. In the United States, we might describe it as corporate farming.

It is safe to say that 90 percent of the Western world has a totally erroneous conception of the Commune (as we did on arrival). The Commune, which is the basic organizational unit of Chinese agriculture, actually doesn't do much farming. The farming is done by Production Teams, such as we were visiting at Shuang Wang, or by larger concentrations or combinations of Production Teams known as Production Brigades. The Shuang Wang Commune has 11 brigades; the brigade of which this Production Team is a part, has 356 families with 1,812 people.

The Commune itself is a combination corporate headquarters, industrial center, and shopping center. It must support itself without taxing or taking grain from its member Production Teams. It operates factories and workshops and has some farmland of its own. It also operates the hospital and middle schools. Primary schools are operated by the brigades. In Shuang Wang Commune, there are 13 primary schools and 4 middle schools. The Commune is also expected to render technical and other assistance to help the poorer Production Teams achieve self-sufficiency or improved efficiency.

The Chinese use several terms to describe Production Teams such as that at Shuang Wang. They are "the basic accounting unit," we were told. Or again, this is where "collective ownership now exists." Theoretically, ownership will eventually be transferred to the Commune (and thus to the state), but the Chinese themselves admit that, for any foreseeable future, these collective villages are likely to hang on to the title to their lands as well as to the small private plots each family has been granted in a concession to individual enterprise.

As we walked through the farmlands of Shuang Wang, we saw several examples in action of Mao's slogan of "Walking on Two Legs." In one field, a girl picked cotton while stepping gingerly to avoid the small green shafts of wheat already planted in the same field. Across the road, rows of tall green onions were growing between the fruit trees in the orchard. In the fields, two large tractors plowed the ground, followed by ox-drawn harrows and by lines of men and women with foot-wide hoes who leveled the ground and pushed up the small ridges used for irrigation channels.

In the farmyard, pigs slept in pens made of mud brick with Mao

Threshing floor is site of community activity as all ages participate. Here corn is shelled. Later both rice and wheat are threshed on the hard clay surface.

Neat pigsty of mud brick with architectural decoration is pride of Shuang Wang Production Team. Signs exhort peasants to greater pig production to better serve the state.

slogans painted on the walls above their heads. The pens were as clean and as carefully tended as American dairy barns. Some pigs had long snouts and thin shanks, but fat black pigs with short noses in other pens would have been showpieces at an American county fair.

The barnyard, except for the primitive stone turntable for grinding grain, was much like its American counterpart. Steers and bulls were tethered in one area, while around the corner, cows with Holstein markings, but with big haunches and small udders, munched hungrily on dry fodder.

All of this represented a measure of affluence unknown to any of these families (except the landlords) only two decades ago. In our morning conversation with the chairman of the Revolutionary Committee which governs Shuang Wang, he told us that the Shuang Wang Production Team has 73 bicycles, 22 sewing machines, and 30 radios and that 80 percent of the families have either watches or clocks. Every family in the village lives in a house built since 1955. More astonishing is the fact that almost 70 percent of the families have some savings in the Commune bank. (This provides the capital to buy machinery, as well as about a 4 percent rate of interest to the saver.) The former landlords, who survived the executions we saw portrayed in several revolutionary ballets, have now been "reeducated," we were told, and work alongside the peasants.

Income to members is distributed on the basis of work points. The minimum per day for a man is ten work points, but the women, who seemed to be working just as hard as the men, get a minimum of only seven or eight work points. Skilled workers get higher pay; a tractor driver, for example, gets 15 work points per day.

The houses of Shuang Wang are deceptive. Walking down the street, we saw only high adobe walls, with tall stalks of corn fodder (used for fuel) alongside each entryway. These walls, made of the same hard clay from which China wrests its food, are as durable as concrete. In some parts of China, these straw-and-adobe structures are painted white; here in sunny Shensi Province, they are allowed to retain their natural color.

After our tour of the fields, we had lunch with Li Hsin-chai and his wife, Pei Chin-shih. He is 43 and she is 45. At lunch we were joined by their 22-year-old daughter, who had come home to help on this special occasion. Li is a worker in the fields, and though not a member of the Revolutionary Committee, he is a man of substance in the village. We entered the gate in the wall, which gives his house privacy from the streets, and walked into a small courtyard, where chickens scurried about. On our right was a room filled with corn,

Li Hsin-chai, Shuang Wang peasant, who took the author home for lunch.

grain, and jars of preserved food in an arrangement that might have served well as the background of a Grant Wood painting.

After passing through this dirt courtyard, we entered a small atrium open to the sky, with brick flooring and a drain in the center. Later we were to learn that this was where they captured their rainwater.

Traditional Chinese doors of wood and parchment windows opened into a fair-sized room with a table and four benches. To the right, Pei Chin-shih and her daughter were at work over two black stoves in a roomy kitchen with two large pans hanging on the wall.

The ceiling in the room arched high over our heads, supported by round beams the size of telephone poles. The whole ceiling was blackened by charcoal and wood smoke from the two stoves in the kitchen.

There was a bedroom at either side of the central room, each with a brick *kang,* the style of bed used in northern China. Essentially, a *kang* looks like a fireplace chimney lying on its side and is just as hard. A fire in a small fireplace or brick stove, usually next to the bed rather than under it, sends its smoke and heat circulating under the bed before it goes up the chimney. Neatly folded comforters were stacked in each corner of the *kang,* whose brick surface was covered by a single cotton coverlet.

An old-fashioned white enamel basin stood at one side of the central room, and after our hostess had assured herself that the water was just the right temperature, we were invited to wash up. We wiped our hands on the customary Chinese wet towel, which hung just above the basin.

Besides myself, there were three other guests for lunch—Charles Bennett of Oklahoma City, Charles Rowe of Fredericksburg, Virginia, and our interpreter, Yeh Chin. When we took our places at the table, Pei Chin-shih, in peasant black and wearing the traditional towel on her head, handed each of us a sweet potato. At this moment, there were not even chopsticks on the table, so I waited to see what our host would do (which is the same way I learned to eat an artichoke at home). He picked up the yam, peeled it with his hands, and ate it as we would a banana, putting the peelings on the wooden top of the table. Then when he finished, he stood up, brought a wet cloth from the kitchen, and helped his wife by cleaning up all our peelings. It was very efficient, and as much teamwork as Gloria Steinem could have wanted.

While we men were eating our yams, the two women had been busy in the kitchen and now brought out a large wooden tray almost as big as the table. It contained three varieties of wheat

Modern caterpillar-tread tractor plowing field alongside harrow pulled by oxen exemplifies the slogan "Walking on Two Legs."

Dry beans are crushed from husks by methods used for thousands of years.

noodles, a bowl full of scrambled eggs, some Chinese pancakes similar to tortillas, a large stack of steamed buns, and a salad of shredded kale (cabbage). Using our chopsticks, we took what we wanted, family style, rolled the food up in our Chinese tortillas, and ate as we would tacos. It was delicious.

After what had already seemed an enormous meal (the Chinese eat their principal meal at midday), we were each offered red soup made of corn and millet in a bowl the size of a vegetable dish. The soup was rather flat-tasting to the palate, but even if it had been nectar, we could not have eaten another spoonful. All of this, of course, was served with delicious green tea.

After lunch, we were invited to wash up again and then to look over the rest of our host's home. (Mike Ogden of Providence, Rhode Island, went to another house for lunch, and after finishing, was handed a cup of warm water, which he took to be a finger bowl. "No," motioned the hostess. Then picking up her own cup, she rinsed the water around in her mouth and spit it out on the dirt floor!)

Washed up and refreshed, we walked out into a backyard shaded by two date trees. Our host, a field worker, told us he had received 1,200 yuan ($516) in 1971, of which 800 yuan was in cash and 400 in grain and cotton. Among other pioneer aspects of the house were two crude spinning wheels standing in the courtyard, where the family spun its own thread from its cotton allocation.

Our host told us that much of the food we had eaten came from his private plot of about a *mou* (one-sixth of an acre), where last year he grew three different crops of kale, potatoes, and other vegetables. His own farm implements hung from the back of the house. In the back courtyard, set off in a corner behind a high clay wall, was the usual rural privy, open to the sky.

The family of Li Hsin-chai no longer worries about starvation or privation. They have a bicycle, a radio, and a loudspeaker, which is connected to the village headquarters and which offers entertainment as well as propaganda.

Their life is primitive by American standards, but it far exceeds the expectations of the world into which they were born as children of poor peasant families. Charles Bennett from Oklahoma, where traces of frontier life are still to be found, put it well: "It may be far less than what we have today," he said, "but it's a lot better than what our pioneers had less than a century ago."

7

Water for the Fields of China

Prior to 1960, it was possible to live and die in Lin Hsien County, in the Tai-hang Mountain area of Honan Province, without ever having seen a fish. Today, fish is a staple of the diet in this mountainous country.

Fish, of course, are merely a corollary benefit of what has been the most visible, the most permanent, and the most dramatic of the achievements of the new China—the irrigation of its lands.

Among the many "big-character" billboards we saw throughout China, one of the slogans which appeared most frequently was "In Agriculture, Learn From Tachai," where an irrigation project was dramatically successful.

Tachai is an isolated country village in the rock-strewn mountains in Shansi Province of North China. In 1953, it was organized as an agricultural cooperative. Today the village is a successful and self-contained agricultural Production Brigade.

The drama of Tachai is not only that its people conquered an unfriendly environment, but that they persevered in the face of a series of catastrophes which read like the Book of Job.

Among the setbacks: In both 1955 and 1957, floods washed out 38 stone embankments, which had been laboriously constructed by hand the previous winter. In 1963, a biblical seven days and seven nights of rain washed out 80 percent of the housing in the village as well as 100 embankments and the fields they supported.

Like proud pioneers, the people of Tachai refused emergency-relief help or funds from the central government and started rebuilding. Today the embankments stand, and aerial cableways and

Water pours through water gates at junction of Heroes Canal
and Red Flag Canal in Lin Hsien.

carts have replaced shoulder poles and donkeys as the means of transporting fertilizer and water to the terraces high up on the hills.

The Chinese attribute this success to the power of "Mao thought." An outsider would more probably ascribe it to a strong local leader with the power to motivate those around him, whatever the dogma.

In Lin Hsien County, it is the Red Flag Canal that has transformed the life of the people. This canal was almost literally torn from the mountains by hand. With sledgehammers, iron spikes, and dynamite manufactured in a factory built by the county and with a labor force that on some days totaled 30,000 people, the peasants cut across 1,250 rocky peaks, drilled 134 tunnels, and built 150 aqueducts of varying sizes until they had created a canal 1,500 kilometers (937 miles) long. Today it brings water (and fish) from the Chang Ho (river) in neighboring Shansi Province to irrigate the fields of Lin Hsien.

Most impressively, all of this was accomplished without the use of a single piece of machinery. Every stone was chiseled and squared by hand. Mammoth stones were lifted into place by levers and cranes hewn from nearby timbers, using techniques dating back thousands of years. In a documentary film tracing the construction of the canal, we saw workmen lowered over the cliff by ropes. While suspended in space, one worker held a spike, and two others swung their sledges to hammer holes for the dynamite. One of those we saw setting the dynamite charge and then being hauled to safety was a young girl, Han Yun-ti, then 18, who headed a team of teen-age girls nicknamed the "Iron Lasses." She is now 24, and when we met her, we found her to have the face of a cherub. Others were not as lucky as Han Yun-ti; the architect who designed the path and structure of the canal was killed by a rockslide following a blasting attempt in one of the tunnels.

Today, small hydroelectric plants dot the hillsides and bring electricity as well as water to the county. The floods and the barren years of drought are now only memories to the 200,000 different people who at one time or another had a hand in the ten-year struggle to build the Red Flag Canal.

Among other benefits, the canal has now made it possible to switch many fields from wheat to rice, a real advantage in this country where the soil is saturated with alkali, which, when it rises to the surface, kills crops that are farmed dry. The water in the rice fields keeps the alkali well below the surface.

Impressive? Yes.

Then I met Mao Miao-sheng in the village of the Ta Tsai-yuan

Han Yun-ti, now 24, was 18 when she headed
team of "Iron Lasses" who helped blast water tunnels
through mountains in Lin Hsien.

(Big Vegetable Garden) Production Brigade in Lin Hsien. All we had been seeing, all we had been learning, and much of what we had been told came together in this one man's life.

The way I met Mao is significant. We had stopped on the dirt road outside the brigade's village and were invited to walk down the street, enter any house, and talk (with the aid of the interpreter) to anyone we wanted. I was fortunate to be in the company of Yao Wei, the interpreter whom Joseph Alsop later was to describe accurately as "the most ideal traveling companion" that either Alsop or his wife had ever encountered.

At first I tried to get some assistance from Yao Wei. "How about this one?" I asked. "Or that one?" But he was determined that nothing be done to suggest the interview was rigged, so he would only say, "Wherever you wish." Finally, I saw some children outside the double wooden doors of a house (or rather the traditional external wall) and plunged in. I was lucky. For I had come upon the household of Mao Miao-sheng, whose narrative of his life is a "One Man's Family" saga of the old and new China. Cynics may say that his story was rehearsed or his experiences taken from fiction, but my colleagues visited ten other households, and none of them heard a story quite like it.

Mao (the name is common and bears no relationship to Chairman Mao) told us that he had been born the son of a poor peasant and that because his family had been unable to feed him, he had been indentured to work for the family of a landlord in the area. When he was 16 (1943), a Chinese recruiter passed through the village, seeking labor for the coal mines of Manchuria (then under Japanese control and called Manchukuo, now the provinces of Liaoning, Kirin, and Heilungkiang). Mao and some others were told that they were being taken to a place where there would be plenty of food and conditions would be better. Actually, the Chinese quisling was paying the landlord a bonus provided by the Japanese to furnish slave labor for the coal mines they were operating in occupied territory. Young Mao was kept prisoner there, working in a deep-shaft coal mine, even after the Japanese surrender. When the Communists took control in 1949, he was able to return to his home county.

His situation today can be described as prosperous, as well as happy. He and his family—four children, two daughters-in-law, and two grandchildren—live in three brick and white-plaster adobe houses on a plot of land about 70 feet by 70 feet.

The house in which Mao and his wife live is about 33 feet by 18 feet. In the courtyard is a kitchen building shaded by an arbor of bean vines. Strings of yellow corn were drying on either side of the yard, and a fat pig slept contentedly in a small pen next to the mud-walled open toilet.

The house itself is divided into one large room, with a concrete shelf and board for kneading dough (some unfinished wheat noodles were in a basket), and a second smaller room about 10 feet by 15 feet, where two large brick *kangs* were erected against either wall, with the small fireplace to heat them in the center.

In a farmer's terms, Mao told us what the conversion to collective farming and eventually the canal had meant to him. Before 1949, the average yield per *mou* (one-sixth of an acre) was about 90 *catties* (about 120 pounds) of grain. After Liberation, the yield rose to 200 *catties* per *mou;* with the introduction of irrigation from the canal, it has now reached 500 to 600 *catties* per *mou.* Added to this is the knowledge that the floods which formerly ravaged the area are now unlikely to occur.

When we asked Mao about his hopes for his children, he gave us the customary answer. "I want them to stay in the village, because I think it is a good life." Then after a pause, he added, "Unless, of course, the state would have need of their services in the factory. Then they would go where they are needed." The last comment reflects, I suspect, what they are told in the political indoctrination courses he and his family attend once each week.

All the houses in the village we visited were built around court-yards, with closed walls and open-air foyers leading to the wooden doors that shut the houses off from the street. There were no locks.

At one dwelling, we found only an old woman, her pinched feet evidence that they had once been bound in the old tradition. She did not want to talk, though she was shy rather than unfriendly, and we respected her wishes.

Next door, we encountered a compound where two brothers lived with their families. One brother was in the fields, and the other was preparing dinner in the compound's kitchen. They were not self-conscious about the fact that the man was preparing the family meal, while the mother did other chores and the daughter looked after her babies.

Yao Wei told us that the new buildings of the compound had been constructed around the yard of the old landlord's house, the large house in which one of the families was living. Here we saw more finished furniture than we had seen in all the previous homes combined.

These families were not only prosperous, but had time to plant and tend the flowers that bloomed in the entryway. If it had not been for the dirt street and the corn drying on the road outside, this might have been the patio of a $100,000 Spanish-style home in a Chicago suburb. That illusion vanished when we entered the court-yard, but still we could see that these were successful people—poised, aware, and friendly.

The grandmother, Wei Chi-hua, wore the traditional floor-length plain black cotton dress still favored by many of the older genera-tion who no longer work actively in the factories and fields. With a pink sash around her waist, she had achieved a certain amount of chic, despite the plain material. The 23-year-old mother, Shih Ho-yun, quietly put her babies to sleep and then came out to join the conversation. This family had a better education than most. Both brothers were primary-school graduates, and one of them had been to middle school.

Lin Hsien is an impressive case study of how the new emphasis on collective agriculture is working. Under the Chinese system, cer-tain major projects are reserved for the central government, but irri-gation and agricultural objectives are the responsibilities of the in-dividual counties and sometimes Communes. Very few of us were prepared for the size of the Commune operation. The Production Brigade we visited, for example, is part of a Commune consisting of 42 different brigades, totaling 80,000 people—certainly a large-scale farming operation by any standard.

The counties are also encouraged (or permitted) to establish the "Five Smalls," or five small industries, which they may initiate with-out clearance with a central authority. These projects vary slightly, depending on the resources in a given area. Almost all counties, however, will have a chemical fertilizer plant and a workshop for repairs of machinery. In Lin Hsien, for example, the "Five Smalls" are: (1) small fertilizer plant; (2) water-conservation works (canals, 25 small hydroelectric power plants); (3) two medium-sized iron and steel plants (to which we saw them hauling ore by modern dump truck and the coal for the furnaces in hand carts and donkey carts); (4) small coal mine; and (5) small workshop for repairs of machinery.

Later in our trip, I was to see other examples of the stress on self-reliance and self-sufficiency when we visited the Ho Lan Production Brigade near the resort city of Wu Xi. The 3,926 people of Ho Lan had literally created a miniconglomerate of agriculture.

The wall-to-wall houses of the brigade stand among broad fields, where two crops of rice and one of wheat are harvested each year. Nearer the houses are fields of mulberry trees, whose leaves feed the silkworms that are cultivated commercially in six-foot-diameter

The lives of Wei Chi-hua, in traditional dress, and her family, who live in the village of the Big Vegetable Garden Production Brigade, have been transformed by China's irrigation program.

A peasant stands proudly before Red Flag Canal in Lin Hsien, which he and 200,000 others helped build over a ten-year period.

wicker trays. In another direction, we walked along the dikes surrounding a series of ponds. Here are raised fish for sale to the mar-
kets as well as coreless pearls, which are ground up and used in
medicines.

The Production Brigade produces its own medicines from herbs
that grow in another field and form the basis of ancient Chinese
tonics and cures we saw brewing in a room full of waist-high
earthen jars. It is really astonishing to see medicine being produced
in a long series of one-story farm buildings; but by this time in the
tour, we had developed such confidence in Chinese medicine that
we popped the proffered samples into our mouths without a moment's hesitation.

Next to the rooms in which the medicines were being manufactured and bottled was a well-lighted room where about 15 women
were busy at rows of sewing machines, producing machine-stitched
embroidery. Most of it would be used for export, they said. And in
still another room of the long farm building, we found a group of
men and women cutting leather for shoes and stitching the pieces
together.

The industriousness of the Chinese people is a legend in the Far
East. In many cities I had visited in past years in various parts of
Asia, the Chinese were often described by the local citizens as un-
scrupulous competitors. The feeling against the Chinese in Malaysia,
for example, is a bitter and continuing fact of political life in that
area.

As I drove along the roads of China and watched the Chinese
people at work in the fields, I saw nothing to suggest that this industriousness has been lessened in any way by their Communist
government.

To a visitor bouncing along a primitive road in a rickety bus, it
appears as if each person is engaged in a highly personal, titanic
struggle with nature. The Chinese attack the ground with hoe,
spade, pickax, wooden plow, or in the case of the children, by fill-
ing their little baskets with their bare hands. When they have machinery pulled by caterpillar-tread tractors, they use that; if not
tractors, then oxen or donkeys or horses; if no animals, then they
themselves in groups of five or more will put a rope over a small
white shoulder pad and pull the plow. Many times, we saw two men
pulling a harrow about six feet wide down a field.

We were fortunate to be in China during the busiest season of the
year—the rice was being harvested, the beans threshed from their
pods, cotton picked, corn being run through the shellers or drying

along the houses or on the roofs, and the compost night soil being dumped in pile after pile on the harvested fields to provide nourishment for the next year's crop.

All China was at work; even the children were released from school to help with the harvest as was once the case in the United States (and still is in certain fruit-growing areas where crops are extremely perishable). But the people of China have always worked, even if only with a crude stick that could barely scratch the soil. The difference today is more than organization—it is hope borne on the waters of the irrigation channels that run along almost every field. For the first time in history, a generation of Chinese are able to sow with the full expectation that there will be a harvest.

8

If You Lived in China...

If you were born in China today, you would find that much of your life was already planned for you at the moment of your birth—and even slightly before.

Your mother would have received free medical care if she worked in a factory, and shortly before your birth, would have begun the 56-day maternity leave to which she was entitled. A doctor would probably help you into the world.

If your mother lived in a rural area, her medical care would have been prepaid out of the approximately $2 per year your family paid into the Commune's welfare fund. And although a "barefoot doctor" might have checked on her health during pregnancy, it would be a traditional Chinese midwife who would help your mother through your birth.

At the end of 56 days, your mother would return to her job, probably taking you with her to the factory nursery. She would not stay home to take care of you, because in China today, she is taught that everyone must serve the state through productive labor if China is to prosper. If your grandmother or grandfather happened to be alive, the chances are they would be sharing your parents' apartment, and in that case, you would be under their care while your mother was away at the factory.

At the age of three, you would be considered beyond the point of infancy and would be enrolled in the nursery kindergarten associated with every large factory, workers' residential center, or Commune. Again, if there were a grandparent at home, you might go home evenings; if not, you would spend six days of the week at school as a live-in student, spending each night in one of the two-foot-by-four-foot, brightly painted cribs standing head to toe in several of the rooms around the nursery courtyard.

In the nursery, you would learn to play games and to sing in unison songs about "Mao chew see" (Chairman Mao), who, you would be told, was the man whose thoughts and simple sayings should govern your whole life. And the red banner of China would be part of the games you played—the races and the contests.

The first stories you would hear would be about heroes and heroines of the Revolution and "socialist reconstruction." One of your most popular songs (as I was to learn on my journey) would have these words: "We're little red soldiers. We listen to Chairman Mao's every word. We want to be revolutionaries even while we're young. We want to be workers, peasants, soldiers when we grow up."

You would remain in your nursery-kindergarten until the age of seven. This wouldn't properly be called "school" even though at the age of five you might start learning some simple words; you would be taught words rather than letters because in Chinese each character is a word. You would also learn to count, but because Chairman Mao wants China to be as modern as possible, you would learn to count in Western-style numerals (and these would be used to keep score at table-tennis matches you and your parents attend and to mark the price of candy in the candy stores).

At the age of seven, you would enter a real school. Here you would learn reading and writing, much of it with stories about how you can help China become a better country. As you grow older and get into middle school (high school), your math, physics, chemistry, and biology courses are filled with examples relating to practical experience. Language drills will always contain a saying of Mao or Marx or Lenin. Although you may live in Shanghai or Peking, two of the world's largest cities, you will still have to learn about farming, because after graduation, you will be expected to go down to the countryside to augment your formal education by what Chairman Mao calls "learning from the masses."

Your education will also contain some practical experience, because with some of your friends, both boys and girls, you will be given time off each fall and spring to march off to the nearby fields to help with the planting and the harvest. On your back, neatly packed inside a colorful red comforter, will be all the clothes and other things you will need for a stay of up to a month in the homes of the peasants you will be helping.

If you are diligent in your studies, particularly in the sayings of Chairman Mao and the function of the state, you will be admitted to the Red Guards. You will be entitled to wear a small red kerchief

No one is too young to work in China. The rake and basket
are both made entirely from materials provided by the land.

around your neck and to take the position of leader or marshal whenever your class marches from one place to another. You will also serve as volunteer guide and usher on national holidays and at special public events.

When you graduate, however, you must give up your membership in the Red Guards. You are not sure why; you are told that it has something to do with the Cultural Revolution, when the Red Guards did many good things to get rid of bad leaders who followed the "revisionist line" but then did not use "self-criticism" and committed many excesses and caused a lot of damage, which harmed the state. Now there are no Red Guards outside the lower and middle schools. The next step up for you will be membership in the Party—if you can qualify.

Before the Cultural Revolution in 1966, when you were 17, you would have been taking exams to go on to the university. But that is not true any more. Now you must first go to work in a factory or on a farm so that you will learn about people who work with their hands and not forget them after you have received your formal education.

If you are lucky, your job may help you with your education. If you are interested in chemistry, for example, you may be assigned to a petrochemical or plastics plant, where you can learn as you work. But wherever you are assigned, there is only one way to get to the university; that is, to work so hard that your fellow workers will approve your application for entrance to the university and recommend you to the local governing committee who must pass the application on. A large part of the decision, you have been told, will be based on your following "the correct political line," and so you must faithfully attend and participate in the three hours or more of political instruction each week. Only then will you be permitted to take the examination that might qualify you for entrance to the university.

You will not necessarily work in the place you choose or even do the kind of work you choose; you will work where you are needed to serve the state. If you work in a factory, you will work eight hours a day six days per week; Sunday will usually be your day off. Some evenings, you will go to class to learn more about the thoughts of Chairman Mao or about the technical skills of your job, or you may watch television in the workers' clubroom at your plant.

If you are an apprentice, your salary will start at only about 20 yuan per month, which means you must continue to live at home or perhaps in a dormitory for single persons provided by the factory. When you reach the "eighth grade" for workers (the lowest), your salary will be about 40 yuan per month.

For a long time, you will not be thinking about marriage because marriage usually means children. And you have been taught that men should not marry until they are 25 to 28 and women 23 to 25; otherwise, there will be so many people in China that once again there will not be enough food for everybody.

If you are a woman, you know that you are entitled to be treated as an equal under the marriage law decreed in 1950, soon after the founding of the People's Republic. Under the law, all that is required for a marriage is for the two people wanting to marry to register with the government office in the district where they live. Both husband and wife enjoy "equal status in the home," the law states; it also guarantees each "the right to free choice of occupation and free participation in work or social activities." Each also has equal rights in the family property and the right to inherit the other's property, small though it may be in today's China.

The marriage law itself gives you a picture of the traditional social customs in the time of your parents and grandparents by prohibiting "bigamy, concubinage, child betrothal, interference with the remarriage of widows, and the exaction of money or gifts in connection with marriages."

The law includes a section on the rights of children. Although you are told there is almost no premarital or extramarital sex in China today, it was considered necessary when the law was passed 23 years ago to extend the same rights to children born out of wedlock as to those born of legal marriages. If the paternity of the child can be established, the father must bear the full cost of his support until the child is 18.

The law allows for divorce, although these are rare in China and are considered not to be in the interest of the state. The women have more protection in divorce than women have in the United States. A husband is not permitted to divorce his pregnant wife, for example, and, in fact, cannot divorce her until a year after the child is born.

Property settlements are arranged by the court when the parties cannot agree, with one of the unusual provisions being that "the principle of benefiting the development of production" should be taken into consideration when settling questions of property division.

If there is a death in your family, there may be a short memorial service attended by fellow workers. But there will be no funeral and no burial. If you become a member of the Communist Party, you will be required to sign an agreement committing your body to cremation. Even if you are not a Party member, you will be reminded often in your classes on "political consciousness" that land is too precious to be set aside for the dead.

After your marriage, if you are lucky, you will move into an apartment assigned to you by the state; otherwise, you may go to live with your parents or your wife's parents. If you live in one of the "new cities" of China, the chances are you will be living in new workers' housing, built by the factory where you work.

In the older and larger cities like Shanghai and Peking, you will be assigned to a "workers' village" with other workers from comparable industries and with similar income levels. If you lived in Tien Shan Workers Village in Shanghai, for instance, most of your neighbors would be workers from steel, oil, or petrochemical plants. If you were Soong Wen-hua of the Canton branch of the China Travel Service, whom we met at Shumchun when we crossed the border, you would be living in an apartment building in Canton where all the other families in the building were also employees of the China Travel Service.

If you have special skills, which put you in the middle grade of workers, you will probably have saved enough while you were single to buy a bicycle (about 150 yuan), and you will probably ride it to work—in part to keep you in shape for the calisthenics that are among the required activities at your factory (your children do the required exercises at their school). But if you live some distance from work, you may commute with a bus ticket that costs you 50¢ a month.

You will pay no income tax as an individual, because the state takes its taxes as a percentage of the output of the factory where you work. The only tax you pay will be a small registration fee for your bicycle—partially so the government can keep track of their numbers, for there are 1,700,000 bicycles in Peking alone.

Your apartment will usually be only one room, and you will share the cooking and toilet facilities with two or three—or sometimes as many as a half-dozen—families on the same floor. If your parents live with you, the state will try to get you a second room, but when the children start to come, they will have to adapt themselves to whatever space can be made for them in one room.

Your rooms look crowded to an American. Your bed is in one corner, a small card-table-sized dining table is in the center of the room, and several straight chairs—usually in a standard maroon mahogany finish—stand against the wall. Beneath the bed and in racks on the walls, you will stow the chests that hold your most precious belongings and your clothes (few apartments have closets or wardrobes).

Chinese family unity is symbolized
by traditional picture taking.

From the ceiling hangs a small electric light (about 40 watts). Utilities are expensive. In some cases, the cost of electricity, gas, and water totals almost as much as your very low rent (about 6 to 8 yuan), which is fixed by the state.

If you are prosperous, your room could also contain a sewing machine and a radio, possibly with a shortwave band. It might even have a long fluorescent light, much brighter than many of your neighbors' lights, suspended without a fixture from two electric cords hanging from the ceiling. The sewing machine costs about $50 to $60, the radio about the same.

In your room there would also be at least one or two tea canisters for that occasional cup of tea you will want during the day. (To make the tea, you take the lid from the juglike teacup that is a fixture of all Chinese households and pour the hot—not boiling— water over the green tea leaves you have placed in the bottom of the cup.)

In the evening, you might go to a movie, even though you know the bill may not have changed for months. If it has changed, you know that it will not be a frivolous evening. The picture will tell a story of modern heroes of the Revolution and how they are either fighting a "revisionist line" or helping to increase production for the benefit of the state.

You will be on the alert at the factory or in reading the *People's Daily* for announcements of sports events, particularly Ping-Pong (you aren't self-conscious about not calling it table tennis) or basketball. In Peking, you might get tickets to an evening's entertainment at the 18,000-seat Capital Gymnasium, where a typical program might include gymnastics, Ping-Pong or volleyball, acrobatics, and a basketball match—all on the same night.

Soccer is also popular, and tickets for a match at the 100,000-seat Workers' Stadium in Peking are not too hard to get. In China, there is no firm line between professional and amateur athletics. The best of the athletes are recruited for the Physical Culture Institute in Peking, a showplace for the best performers in gymnastics, swimming, volleyball, basketball, and badminton.

If you live away from one of the large cities, you watch the bulletin board at the Commune center or local workers' clubs for the traveling ballet groups, acrobatic teams, theater groups—or even propaganda teams, who put on special evenings of entertainment.

Many evenings you and your wife simply go out for a promenade through the nearby shopping center or park, knowing you are walking on the safest streets in the world. A holdup would be almost impossible to execute in a country where almost everything has been reduced to a single norm and where "political consciousness" has taught everyone that he or she is responsible not only for his own welfare, but for the welfare of his neighbors.

One of the things you and your wife might talk about is raising a family, for you would have received family-planning counseling at the factory clinic as soon as you were married. You would also have become eligible for the contraceptives and birth-control pills that are available free to married workers. You have been told that the state is best served if you have no more than two children, but the decision on the final number can wait. You make the decision to start your family now.

Thus, you will have started a new cycle of life in a society much different from that of your parents or grandparents. You are part of a young nation in which two-thirds of all the people are under 30 and half are under 18. As Charles Bennett pointed out to us, that "half under 18" group is twice as many people as there are in the United States.

For you and for them, Mao has flattened out the inequalities of the old society and made it possible for the first time in China's history for no one to be hungry. But the young have many hungers, and these are not all satisfied by rice in the bowl or steamed buns in the oven.

You and your friends have learned faithfully the saying of Chairman Mao that "to serve the state" is the highest goal in life and its most satisfying reward. But if the state changes—as it has with its new rapport with the West and interest in modern technology— then perhaps the nature of "service to the state" may also change.

Will you be trained to work at a machine instead of in the fields? Will your wife wear a dress of gaily colored print as women from other countries do in the newsreel clips she sees on television? Will the broad boulevards of Peking be crowded with automobiles as well as with bicycles?

These are the questions that confront your generation. Your parents had little to fear from revolution because they had so little to lose; your choice is more difficult, for you must pursue the new, knowing you cannot afford to lose what has already been gained.

9

In the Factories, Among the Cadres

The sound of the looms was deafening. I was walking through the principal weaving area of Textile Plant No. 4 near Sian, and the sound of 1,000 shuttles being slammed into place hammered at my ears until I wanted to break into a run for the exit at the opposite end of the room. But amidst this clatter stood a half-dozen Chinese workers in smocks and face masks, placidly observing and supervising the operation.

Textile Plant No. 4—with no brand names to promote, the Chinese see little reason to name their factories—is located in a suburban setting half an hour's drive from the center of Sian. It is a massive plant, whose operations, as well as the living quarters of its workers, reflect the philosophy of the new China and the practical limitations that philosophy imposes on the technical development of its industries.

It was at this plant that we met Kuan Pao-ling, an impressive executive with an air of authority, whose tailored gray Mao suit with its delicate herringbone weave was as handsome as anything we were to see in all China. Kuan's current title is chairman of the Revolutionary Committee that operates the plant; but he was the chief executive before the Revolutionary Committee was formed, and one suspects he would remain the chief executive of this plant, with its 6,400 employees, regardless of how the Communists might restructure the plant's management.

Textile Plant No. 4 is a relatively new factory. Kuan told us that the machinery, manufactured in China, is based on designs derived from a mixture of the Japanese, British, and American equipment that had been imported and used prior to 1949. The plant could not be described as automated, but it was highly mechanized.

The manufacturing process, using a total of 130,000 spindles and 3,240 looms, produces seven kinds of cotton material from raw cotton delivered at the dock. The production quota is set by the state, but the plant can make its own decisions about the grades and the quality of material it will produce.

In the course of a long conversation with Kuan, we tried to ascertain if there were material production incentives, as the walls were covered with the Chinese equivalent of American motivational posters (one showed a goal in terms of rockets headed for the moon —one of the few evidences that the ordinary Chinese were aware of our space program). On other walls were blackboards with production quotas and performance charts.

The rewards, the chairman insisted, were only in the form of prestige, recognition from fellow workers, and a "higher political consciousness" in serving the state, usually certified by achievement awards (some of which we later saw hanging on the wall of a steelworker's apartment in Shanghai).

Some workers received extra ration allotments for meat, cooking oils, and sugar, but these were unrelated to production performance, being reserved for those working in high-temperature drying areas.

We asked equally penetrating questions about the chairman himself. Did he receive special perquisites through his position? Extra pay? The use of an automobile or special quarters as in the Soviet Union? The answer to all these questions was in the negative. The plant had only one automobile, and it was often used as a part-time ambulance. Kuan lived in a small apartment in the workers' village next to the factory. His pay was 255 yuan per month, less than the top pay for a highly skilled worker with seniority within his own factory.

Under the present Chinese system, the Revolutionary Committee at the factory is responsible not only for the working conditions of the employees, but for their living conditions and health care as well. All the workers live in a nearby housing development, which contains both family units and separate dormitories for single men and women. The worker is within a five-minute walk of his job. When the shifts at the plant change, the street is alive with streams of people going from and coming to work.

We were permitted to wander at will through the housing development, located in a series of squares lined with young aspen trees. On a typical floor, four or five family units shared a kitchen less

One-room apartment for parents and two children is typical of housing provided for workers by Sian textile plant.

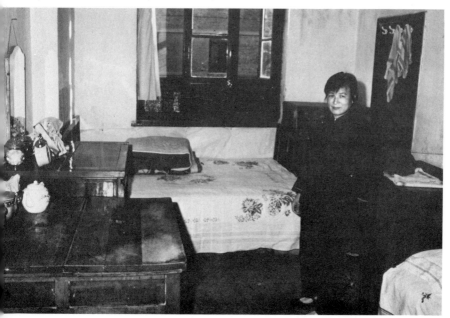

than eight feet square and a toilet facility of about equal dimensions. The only bathing facilities were central bathhouses located throughout the complex. As we had found elsewhere, one family unit, regardless of size, had one room; but a family unit of three generations (parents, children, and grandparents), regardless of numbers, had two rooms. I visited one family in which grandmother, grandfather, and two children slept in one room of the two-room apartment and the parents, the three-year-old, and the oldest child slept in the other. There are no living rooms or sitting rooms as such, only what we would call a bedroom.

The Chinese let us choose apartments to visit at random—they are much more subtle than the Russians about these things—and our group split up about seven ways. But apparently the word had been passed, and every apartment in the place seemed to have been freshly scrubbed. At the apartment we chose on the second floor, the wife had tea ready. How did she know we were going to choose her building or her apartment? Amazing.

In the grandparents' room were two double beds and a dresser. A very large double bed and a three-quarter-sized bed were in the main room. A table with the tea canisters was between the beds. On the opposite wall were two bureaus, a small polished walnut chest, a small metal trunk, and a sewing machine—an integral part of every substantial Chinese household. A large radio was on top of one of the bureaus.

In another apartment on the same floor, we were cordially received by another woman who works in the factory; her husband works in the Textile Research Institute. He makes 80 yuan; she makes 60. Their rent is 4 yuan per month. They had a small transistor radio in the window. The only light was from a single naked bulb hanging from the ceiling.

The kitchen consisted of a sink about two feet wide and a small potbellied, charcoal-burning iron stove. There is a toilet on the floor, but we saw no bathing facilities. For recreation, we were told, they usually go to the movies or opera every Saturday night. Sunday is frequently spent shopping. Neither family had a bicycle; they said they lived so close to the plant they had no use for one.

Health care is provided at several clinics within the factory and housing development as well as at a central hospital. To take care of about 15,000 people, the factory employs 22 doctors, an equal number of nurses, as well as about 20 "small doctors," or paramedics. The factory is not only required to provide health services, but must operate in a way to produce capital for any of the facilities needed to take care of the factory's work force.

The children of the workers were being cared for at a day nursery and kindergarten, where 500 of the 800 students were six-day live-in boarders who spent only one day per week with their parents. Near the school and near many of the apartments were brick air-raid shelters, which had been carefully dug into the sandy terrain.

The workers' wages are low, starting at 32 yuan per month and averaging only about 60 yuan. However, it must be kept in mind that both husband and wife usually work, which doubles the family income.

In addition to a 48-hour workweek, there are 4½ hours of classes per week, three of these spent in political study and 1½ in technical training.

Pay within each department is decided by the group itself, and then their recommendation is forwarded to the Revolutionary Committee for approval. Some pay suggestions may be disapproved, and all are also subject to criticism by other groups at the same level, which may file a protest. Promotions are accomplished by the same procedure.

In the terminology of the Cultural Revolution, promotions are decided on the basis of: (1) political consciousness; (2) technical skill; and (3) seniority. The mysterious term "political consciousness" means that if you are politically correct, you will work harder because you believe in the state. Thus, when analyzed, promotions are based on hard work, technical skills, and length of service just as in the United States, except that in China nominations for promotion come from below rather than from above.

In keeping with Chairman Mao's admonition to "learn from the masses," Kuan, the chief executive of Textile Plant No. 4, said he spent one day per week alongside the workers. But in reply to our questions, he gave us the impression that much of this time in the plant was actually spent in troubleshooting rather than in a specific production assignment.

All the administrative staff, or cadres, at this plant are required to work 45 days per year on the production line. This device, instituted to comply with Mao's directive that all white-collar workers "learn from the masses," appears to a visitor to be an ingenious solution to the alternative of going to the countryside and working alongside the peasants; it also retains valuable skills within the factories where they can be most productive for China. At other plants, however, we found that many of the white-collar workers and supervisors were required to spend some time at the May 7 schools, set up under a directive issued by Mao.

Mao's famous directive, issued on May 7, 1968—a date perpetuated in the name of the May 7 schools—sought to provide a means for a shared experience between the urban worker and intellectual and the rural peasant. "It is highly necessary," he wrote, "for young people with education to go to the country to be reeducated by the poor and middle-class peasants.

"Going down to do manual labor gives vast numbers of cadres an excellent opportunity to study once again," Mao said in the directive, adding that "this should be done by all cadres except those who are old, weak, ill, or disabled."

The East Is Red May 7 School, located on a sandy plain about 20 miles southwest of Peking, is one of the more notable successes in this intensive program of forcing urban workers and intellectuals to share in the peasant experience and, presumably, through communal living, to learn to substitute group values for those of personal ambition or self-interest.

"Our purpose here," said Chang Hung-fan, 41-year-old spokesman for the school that serves the Chung Wen district, "is to train and temper our students to serve the people heart and soul. The purpose of coming here is to remold one's outlook, to consolidate the dictatorship of the proletariat, to build the motherland and prevent revisionism."

"Train and temper" were the key words in his presentation, and they were repeated with a frequency chilling to his American visitors. One of the most persistent questions asked by some of my colleagues on our 4,000-mile journey through China pertained to this exact point: Has China been able to create a new kind of person—a Mao man—who can exist without the traditional self-motivation that we have always assumed to be part of human nature? Had George Orwell's controlled society of 1984 actually arrived in China a decade earlier?

The Chinese usually evaded the question about whether Mao's teachings had changed human nature, expounding instead on the fact that people were behaving differently today from the way they did under the old regime. The prospect of a change in human nature was of less interest to them than the fact that people were following the "correct line" in their thinking.

Soong Wen-hua, our young escort from Canton, summed it up succinctly. "We cannot say that China has produced a new man in the days since Liberation. But a new society, yes."

In this light, the May 7 schools can be seen as the means by which Mao hopes to surmount the barriers of class, cultural background, and educational differences to produce a consensus—particularly among those charged with leadership roles in China.

Schoolteachers at May 7 school for "tempering" of the mind
and spirit pick turnip leaves in the field.

Huang Hua, China's ambassador to the UN, had been through the tempering process of a May 7 school in 1969, when he and many other diplomats were recalled for reeducation. Yao Wei, our able interpreter, had spent a year in a May 7 school and his wife, a Russian language expert, a longer period.

The technique used to accomplish this process of reeducation and political indoctrination is a combination of manual labor and study. At the East Is Red May 7 School, Chang Hung-fan told us there were three principal areas of reading and discussion: first, the study of Mao, Marx, and Lenin; second, a study of the theories of Engels; and third, the writings of Mao on "contradiction and practice." Reading by the student is augmented by class instruction and seminars amounting to an average of three days every two weeks. Class schedules are adjusted according to the growing season and the amount of work to be done in the fields.

In the East Is Red May 7 School at the time of our visit, there were 540 students, living in clusters of dormitories scattered around the school farm. The farm was once the riverbed of the Yung-ting River, which was finally tamed during the Ching Dynasty and channeled behind high dikes just beyond the edge of the farm. Since the school was started, over 200 acres have been reclaimed from what was once a barren wasteland of undulating sand dunes, some of which could still be seen. The principal crops are rice and peanuts.

The school maintains its own workshops for repairing the few pieces of mechanized equipment. In one workshop, students were building a cabin for the school's oversized tractor so it could be used on days when the cold wind swept across the sandy plain.

Students at the school, among whom we found a high proportion of schoolteachers, usually stay about six months, although we talked with several former administrators who had been there for two years. The students may keep in touch with their families by phone, and since most of them come from the surrounding area, they are allowed to visit home at least once each month. They continue to draw their full salary, paid by the government department by which they were employed and to which they will probably return.

Meanwhile, the students not only learn farming, but add to the manpower pool needed to reclaim every square meter of arable land for China's millions. They also learn other skills. In the kitchen, we found a group of four workers preparing the evening meal for 100 students; two were schoolteachers, and two were white-collar supervisors—none of them had ever cooked before coming to the school.

More than 2,400 people from the district had been through the school since its founding. We were told that most of them—after the proper "tempering"—had been able to return to their old positions. One of the school's success stories described to us was that of a Mr. Shing, who had been head of the health department of the district prior to the Cultural Revolution. Mr. Shing had been one of those officials ridiculed with "big-character" billboards because he refused to go to the countryside as the leader of the medical team to which he had been assigned when Mao called for giving top priority to medical work in rural areas. After the Cultural Revolution, Mr. Shing was assigned to the East Is Red May 7 School, where he remained for two years. He is now back at his old job as head of the health bureau.

Mr. Shing had been assigned to the school, but others have volunteered for the experience. Originally, the May 7 schools were, as humorously described by Edgar Snow, "a reform school for reformers," but recently they have taken on many of the aspects of a leadership training institute. The schools are still committed to reinforcing the ideological commitment of those who normally do not work with their hands. But reward has replaced corrective treatment as the context in which the Chinese perceive the schools. Now there is actually social pressure to get into the schools as a step toward building a better career in this puzzling society with its strong emphasis on the glorification of manual labor.

At the East Is Red May 7 School, our host Chang Hung-fan, told us with pride that within three to five years every cadre in the district would have been through the school or at least would have had the option of enrolling.

We had heard the word "cadre" so much that I decided to ask for a more specific meaning of the word. This produced a lively discussion among the 10 to 12 Chinese present, among whom were 8 Party members. The only way we could approach an understandable definition of the word, which is used to refer both to an individual and to a group, is that a "cadre" is: not a worker . . . not a peasant, unless he is a Production Brigade leader or above . . . not a soldier below the rank of officer. There is a further distinction between "ordinary cadres," which we took to be straw bosses, supervisors, or possibly white-collar workers, and "leading cadres," who are obviously people in positions of authority.

"Cadre" is an interesting example of the way the Chinese have found terms to suit their system, in which rank and class distinctions have probably been as close to being abolished as is humanly possible. In the army, for example, the only distinction between an officer and an enlisted man is that the officer's uniform has four pockets—two at the breast and two at the hips—while the ordinary soldier's has only the two pockets at the breast. If a captain from Canton meets a general from Peking, they must compare identity cards to establish rank. But since saluting has been done away with, it really doesn't make much difference what their rank is.

At the end of the day, our hosts and the cadres among the students invited us to attend a small entertainment in the school auditorium. After a rousing chorus of "Great Peking," which is a tremendous favorite in China's concert halls and on the radio, a group of young teachers executed a simple but charming and well-done dance called "Happy Are the East Is Red May 7 Freedom Fighters Planting Rice." The title conveys the idea that all art and culture has a heavy propaganda theme, which was further demonstrated a few minutes later when the male chorus rendered a roof-raising presentation of "We Shall Liberate Taiwan" for its all-American audience. Then, as quickly, the mood shifted, and we were treated to a Chinese translation of the American spiritual "We Shall Not Be Moved."

As our hosts applauded and we got into our cars for the return drive to Peking, the pleasure in our reception could not quite blot out the realization of how easy it is for governments to "train and temper" the minds of men and women into unreasoning obedience.

10

Three Lives,
but One Life-Style

By educated estimate, there are about 800 million people living in China today. Happily, it was not necessary to meet all of them—or even a significant fraction of them—in order to piece together a picture of life for the average Chinese.

I met, or was present at interviews, with perhaps 100 Chinese, and many of them were quite willing to tell us the story of their lives. Of this number, you will be introduced to only three, but their stories mirror the lives of the tens of millions who live and work in the cities of China.

Li Hsiu-ying

Li Hsiu-ying is a petite, vivacious woman of 40, with shortcropped hair, wide-set eyes, and the square face typical of Chinese from Shanghai. She is the boss and plant manager of a small electrical-parts factory producing ten different kinds of silicon rectifiers for use in transformers.

Ms. Li has come a long way. She was one of five girl-children of extremely poor parents, both of whom were employed in a textile mill—"a capitalist textile mill," in Li's own words. She saw two of her sisters die of starvation and was herself consumptive; but even with her illness, she was put to work in the mill at the age of 12.

At the time of Liberation, she was illiterate. After the change in government, she learned to read and write in the adult-education classes at the textile mill where she was employed, and she partici-pated in the political-education activities as well. She joined the Communist Party in 1952, and since 1953, has been a cadre, or ad-

Li Hsiu-ying, petite manager of a Shanghai
electrical-parts factory employing 270 workers.

ministrator. In terms reminiscent of the May 7 school, she said, "After I was tempered through political education, I became a cadre."

Married, with two young children, she has been in her present post since 1970, when she had asked to be transferred to a smaller plant "to be closer to the masses." Later we learned that she is actually in charge of political education at the plant and that the production responsibility still rests with the former manager, Long Hun-chen, who, in post-Cultural Revolution terminology, is now "vice-chairman of the Revolutionary Committee," while Ms. Li holds the title of chairman.

The wages for the 270 workers in the factory range from 36 yuan to 80 or 90 yuan per month. The chairman makes 74 yuan, and like others we met, considers it proper for skilled workers to make more than administrators. The employees work the usual eight hours a day six days per week. Men retire at 60 and women at 50, usually at about 70 percent of their highest pay. When one of our group said he considered this earlier retirement for women to be discrimination, the woman chairman pooh-poohed the idea. "There are physical differences in the strength of men and woman, and they should be taken into consideration," she said. When the questioner pursued the subject, she dismissed him with the comment that "What you are saying is merely a phenomenon, not the substance." This reply was typical of the kind of philosophical clichés that frequently popped up in ideological exchanges.

The evolution of the factory over which Li Hsiu-ying presides is as interesting as her own story. Ten years ago this same plant, using much of the same machinery, was busy making ornamental glass, principally for lamps, chandeliers, and other decorative objects. Then came the Cultural Revolution and the decision to convert the factory to work that would be of "greater service to the state."

Equipment that was formerly used to grind dewdrop chandelier glass was converted to grinding silicon for rectifiers. Experienced workers were brought in to retrain the employees, and the first prototype of the new rectifiers was produced in 50 days. The entire transition was completed in six months.

Ms. Li told us that every rectifier was unconditionally guaranteed to insure good quality of work. If it is defective, it can be returned, and it will be replaced. Other business practices are comparable to those in the United States, including a recent questionnaire sent to customers asking for suggestions on how service or product quality could be improved.

Because it is a small plant, housing for single workers and others without housing in Shanghai is provided in a nearby workers' village, shared by several factories in the area. Except for five national holidays, there are no vacations, but workers whose families live more than a day's travel (to go and return) from Shanghai are given regular leaves to visit their families.

We were impressed with the ability of this woman, the manager of a small factory, to carry on a discussion and answer questions without any seeming hesitancy at all. When she was asked if there were an official line passed down from Peking on such subjects as changing one's attitude toward the United States, she vigorously denied it. "We don't need an official line," she said. "I personally feel there have been some real changes in the world. And after President Nixon's visit, we were each free to express our own views." Then she threw in this observation: "Also you must remember there have been some changes in President Nixon's views. What we are seeing merely reflects the real change in the world today." She said she was well aware that American workers have better salaries, living conditions, and material possessions than the Chinese worker. But, she cautioned us, comparisons would be wrong because China started from an entirely different foundation.

When asked her reaction to the problem of choosing a successor to Mao, she replied in almost the identical language used by Chou En-lai, another indication of how deep and how widespread the ideological indoctrination is. "We have thousands of leaders," she replied, "and I am sure that whoever is chosen will be someone who has 'been tempered through turmoil.' "

During our interrogation, a young girl in pigtails, who appeared to be about 18 but later told us she was 26, was busy taking notes on every question and answer. After the interview, she was identified as Yuh Hsia, secretary of the Youth Communist League, and we learned that her extensive notes were to be the basis of self-criticism, which must always be part of one's "political consciousness" in this highly politicized environment. She would take her account of the interview to the next meeting of the League, and the members would analyze both questions and answers to determine not only if the answers followed the correct line, but also how they might be improved to present the people's accomplishments in a more effective way.

Lu Tsu-yung

Lu Tsu-yung is 42, a crane operator in a steel plant in Shanghai, and the beneficiary of new public housing. Built by the government for some 17,000 families, the section is called, in Chinese under-

Gas burners in kitchen that Lu Tsu-yung's family
shares with two other families.

Crane operator Lu Tsu-yung and his wife, Shu Hsun-mei,
who works in a chemical factory, sit proudly among their possessions
in Shanghai apartment.

statement, the Tien Shan Workers Village. Actually, it is a complete community of new apartment dwellings erected since 1952 that houses a population of 75,000.

Lu Tsu-yung's household is among the more prosperous we visited, and the housing is superior to that at Textile Plant No. 4 in Sian. He shares a two-room apartment with his wife, Shu Hsun-mei, also 42, who works in a chemical factory; his mother, who was busy in the kitchen; a daughter, 20, who works as an apprentice in a shipyard; and two sons, 17 and 14, who are in middle school.

Their two rooms would be considered 1½ rooms by American standards. One room is about 16 feet square, and the other about 8 feet by 12 feet, just large enough for a double bed and a desk. In the larger room are two beds, a large wardrobe, a high bureau with a chiming clock on top and an attached mirror, the usual three-foot-square table for putting out the meal, and about a half-dozen straight-backed wooden chairs.

All the furniture is finished in a mahogany veneer and is of better quality than any I had seen elsewhere. In the smaller room where the parents sleep are a sewing machine and a desk-top short-wave radio—both marks of prosperity. Above the bed are certificates of outstanding performance earned by Lu in his work as a crane operator.

Across the hall are a bathroom and a kitchen, both of which are shared with two other families on the floor. The bathroom contains a tub of unfinished concrete, and over the sink is a cold-water tap. The toilet is of Western style with a flush box and seat, different from the toilets in Sian, which are at the floor-level, even when made of white enamel. The kitchen would not be recognizable as such in the United States. It consists of only a small work area and three twin-burner gas hot plates, each with its own gas meter.

The family has no bicycle because they can buy commuter tickets on the bus, which takes them to work for about 50¢ per month.

As were other Chinese, Lu was quite relaxed about discussing his personal income and budget. He and his wife have a combined income of 160 yuan per month, and their daughter's apprentice wages add 20 yuan to the family's income. Of this, 7.8 yuan, or 4.3 percent, goes for rent (the highest we have found), and the cost of utilities (they have both a bulb and a fluorescent light) brings this to a total of 15 yuan. They figure 15 yuan, or 8.3 percent, per month per person for food. They spend 30 yuan per year per person on clothing and send 10 yuan per month to the wife's mother in the country. Recreation costs are negligible, and they are saving about 30 yuan per month, almost 16.6 percent of their income.

Both husband and wife were well-dressed in the drab Mao style, and I noticed that he was wearing rayon socks and like-new leather shoes with heavy rubber soles.

Before the new government was established in 1949, neither of these two people had been able to read and write because their parents had not had the money to send them to school. Lu came to Shanghai at 16 to stay with relatives because his poor peasant family did not have enough food for him. Both he and his wife enrolled in the part-time schools provided workers, and both are now literate.

They see TV only in the clubrooms at their respective factories, and their children are able to watch it at school. Most of their news comes from the radio; to our distress, they said they very seldom read a newspaper.

Like the farmer we met in a Commune near Lin Hsien, this Shanghai couple was not particularly concerned with ideology. But what they could demonstrate was that their government had made a new and better life for them and had done it within a single generation.

Liang Wan-chuan

Liang Wan-chuan, 37, is the manager of a plant making a product that no Chinese can buy—automobiles.

Liang's title is vice-chairman of the Shanghai Automobile and Truck Factory. Although he was elected to his present position by his fellow workers, he continues to draw only the salary of a "fourth-grade" worker ($33 per month). Liang speaks with authority about working conditions and production quotas; but for technical questions about manufacturing procedures and costs, he turns to a gray-haired man in his 50s, sitting across the table. Based on our experiences at other factories, we were able to deduce that the older man is the former plant manager (before the Cultural Revolution) and that though he may now have a lesser title, he is still responsible for operations in the plant.

The factory had its origins in a small repair shop formerly run by members of Chiang Kai-shek's Kuomintang (The People's Party, or Nationalists). After the Communists took over, this repair shop was combined with two others, confiscated from foreign owners, and moved to a new location amid broad rice fields half an hour's drive from the center of the city.

During the Great Leap Forward in 1958, the factory started fabricating its own replacement parts and followed this up with a partial assembly-line operation, which produced 500 jeeps. As production skills increased, the factory started manufacturing Shanghai sedans (in which we had been riding on our tours of the cities) and two-

Body assembly line at Shanghai Automobile and
Truck Factory makes limited use of mass-production
techniques. Parts have previously been assembled by hand.

Greater priority given to trucks and work vehicles is evident in contrast
with nonmechanized auto-production line. Plant produces almost
four times as many trucks as autos.

ton pickup trucks. In 1973, the 1,400 workers in the plant will produce about 2,000 trucks and 600 sedans.

Along the road as we drove up to the plant were lines of finished trucks, some of which were being driven away by uniformed soldiers. The Chinese said these were soldier-workers and were merely delivering the trucks to designated government outlets; the trucks were not necessarily destined for the army. We were surprised to learn that in an installation of this size and importance, there were no military members on the Revolutionary Committee in charge.

Liang said that no figures on the relationship between cost and price could be given, because the government would fix the price after the truck was delivered from the factory.

Much of the factory's production can be described as handicraft labor in a factory setting. Most of the machinery we saw in the plant, including the heavy-duty stamping machines, was imported from Eastern Europe—a few pieces of machinery being conspicuously new. For the most part, the shaping, welding, and assembling were done in fixed work areas and the product hand-trundled to a central collection point.

The truck bodies and engines were lowered onto a preassembled chassis-and-wheel assembly by a work force of 28 men, using a gear-and-chain overhead hoist. The line was being operated at low speed because of a shortage of parts, with one finished truck coming off every two hours; when the line operates at full speed, a truck is produced every 50 minutes.

We were told that the sedans, hand-assembled and sitting on wooden sawhorses during production, would soon appear in a new model, with a V-8 engine to replace the present 6-cylinder engine. When asked about the design, the Chinese said it was a collective effort on the "Three-in-One" principle of "worker, technician, and cadre"; but they also added that anyone familiar with a Mercedes 220 would recognize the basic engine and design trim. The body design of the cars seemed to be derived from the Russian Volga, which in turn was derived from American models of the 1930s.

When asked if the new cars would be called '73 models, the Chinese laughed heartily. "If you wish," they replied, "but we expect it will be around quite a long time after 1973." Since the last model change had been in 1958, we got the point.

Liang is also responsible for keeping up the "political consciousness" of the workers. Their interests are represented through a Workers' Congress in the plant, but their demands (one of which was for hard-toed safety shoes) seem rather tame in comparison with those of a union grievance committee in the United States.

Liang admitted that he sometimes had pressure from workers for increased pay, but he attributed this to the "revisionist thinking" of Liu Shao-chi and said it occurred only in minor instances. In fact, almost all the issues Liang faced as manager seemed to involve a mixture of politics and economics; he told us, for example, that the few remaining trouble spots involved ultraleftists, some of whom revealed their tendencies to anarchism by refusing to wear safety glasses as a gesture of protest against all rules. It was one of the rare occasions when dissent was both admitted and identified.

Efficiency is hard to measure in such a setting. The quality of the work in this auto and truck factory, as in the other plants we had visited, seemed to be excellent. Certainly the Shanghai sedans, manufactured in this factory, had performed flawlessly throughout our tour of China.

Industrialist David Packard told Joseph Alsop after Alsop's trip to China: "Industrial rationalization and automation are good investments when labor is scarce and costly; but . . . bad investments where labor is plentiful, skillful, and cheap."

Labor is certainly plentiful in China today, and the government apparently operates on the same philosophy in the factories as it does in the Communes: The cheapest way to get productivity in China is to substitute cheap labor for expensive machinery.

As might be expected, we American visitors asked if the workers did not expect additional pay as their productivity and skills improved. Liang insisted that the desire for additional pay for the best workers was only a minimal problem. "Sometimes people are unhappy about their pay," he conceded, "but through ideological education, we are able to persuade them they must work to serve the people of China and build up the motherland."

At this plant as well as at others, workers are required to spend 4½ hours per week in political and technical study, in addition to their six-day, 48-hour week. Under this system, it will be a long time before Liang Wan-chuan has a leisure-time problem.

11

Shanghai–City Without Sin

Shanghai is different. The traffic moves more briskly, the streets are more crowded, the Mao jackets more tailored, and China's only uniformed policewomen direct traffic in crisp white jackets, which provide dramatic contrast to the twin black braids hanging out from their caps almost to their waists.

The architecture is different too. Elsewhere we have seen the Russian touch, with monumental squares and faceless yellow buildings. Here the British came first and lasted longer. On the Bund along the Whangpoo River, huge piles of British stone are carbons of their counterparts in Whitehall and along the Strand.

From the top-floor dining room of the once-famous Cathay Hotel (now the Peace Hotel), we can see ships of a dozen nations at anchor, while Chinese junks, powered by sail, oar, or sputtering engine, carry cargoes to the riverbanks. But the cargoes of these ships have changed. Once it was heroin, booty, women, intrigue— whatever could be sold in a city where everything, including honor and life, was for sale.

Once boasting of a reputation as a "paradise for sinners," today Shanghai firmly rejects that accolade. The city, which once had the longest bar in the world, has been so thoroughly restructured that now it has no public bar at all. Blood Alley (Rue Chu Pao San), once a street of sailors' brawls and rowdy bars, is now a quiet street where there is neither a song nor a drink to be had. The streets, once among the most dangerous in the world, are so safe that it requires a force of only 1,000 police to keep order, direct traffic, and protect the public safety. This is the new Shanghai, now the largest city in the world.

Shanghai waterfront still shows strong British influence in buildings constructed during occupation.

For the people of Shanghai, the single most important change is the fact that for the first time since 1840, they are the masters of their own city. Prior to 1949, Western nations had been able to bar a Chinese from entering a section of his own city or to charge him a toll if he must enter to work for a foreign master.

Looking down from the Peace Hotel, a Chinese friend pointed to the park where the sign that said "No Chinese or dogs permitted" had stood. Emotion in his voice, he said, "I saw it with my own eyes." Another Chinese friend stood at the rail of the cruise boat taking us up the Whangpoo River and pointed out a small bridge near Shanghai Mansions. "Before Liberation," he told us, "I had to pay a toll to cross that bridge just because I was Chinese. Now I can walk across it as a free man."

At a banquet in the Peace Hotel, Li Hsiu-ying, the factory manager who had been our hostess that day, was caught in an unguarded moment by Bill Hill of the *Washington Star* (now the *Washington Star-News*). "What are you thinking of?" she was asked. "I was thinking," she replied with a friendly laugh, "that before the Liberation, someone like me would never have been allowed to walk through the doors of this hotel."

Bill Hornby of the *Denver Post,* who had been in Shanghai with American troops immediately after World War II, pointed to the places where the Chinese used to sleep in the streets, even in the cold of winter. He commented also on the cleanliness today—no debris, no litter, and no excrement. It is a different city now, but it is also a city living in old shells. The Chinese take no pride in these buildings; they use them, but they do not maintain them. (For the first time we saw cockroaches in our rooms.) It is almost as if the drabness is an encouragement to decay.

As Hornby wrote on his return: "Gone are the rickshaws pulling the man in the white pith helmet. Gone the beggars, the whores in their slit-silk skirts, the hungry kids, the gross inequities of class and wealth between Chinese. And the most poignant tombs in China, those Western skyscrapers standing shabby along the Shanghai waterfront, certify that the foreigner with his hand in the Chinese till is also gone, forever."

The militancy with which the current Chinese leadership viewed the former occupation of their seaport cities by Western powers was forcefully revealed to us when we met Hsu Ching-hsien, deputy mayor of Shanghai.

Hsu Ching-hsien, though only 37, was a paradoxical blend of politician and revolutionary. A bland smile never left his face, but there was the hardness of steel in his answers. He wore a gray Mao suit of elegant material and took total control of the conference. If an American editor interrupted with a question before Hsu concluded his answer, the editor was reprimanded directly and without apology. For the first time, the Chinese in the room outnumbered the members of our own group. We later learned they were local journalists there to watch Hsu perform.

Despite the authority with which Hsu took charge of the conference, he was cordial in welcoming us to his city, saying that the gates of Shanghai were wide open to foreign visitors. He said that they had so many to meet they could hardly get their work done and quoted a Chinese axiom: "Even if you go through Shanghai on horseback, it will take a week." He hoped foreign visitors would gradually increase, Hsu went on, but he used the word "gradually" rather guardedly, or at least so it seemed in translation.

Hsu began his remarks by recalling a cruel night in January, 1945, as it was described in *The Times* of London. A cold northern wind swept over Shanghai and left 800 people dead, most of them among the city's homeless. Many of the dead were found huddled together under discarded newspapers, which they had tried to use for shelters, in the infield of the local racetrack.

By contrast, he said, everyone in Shanghai has been gradually provided with housing since 1949, though he quickly conceded that much of it was not up to standard. (We could testify to this, for in the older parts of Shanghai, we saw several slum areas comparable to those in cities in other countries of Asia—though nothing so bad as India's.) "We know we haven't reached a state of affluence," Hsu said, "but everyone has food, everyone has shelter, and everyone has enough to buy needed clothing, even though it is very plain."

The responsibility for governing this autonomous urban area rests with an enormous Revolutionary Committee of 150 members, which functions as city council, cabinet, and administration. The committee has one chairman—the leading young radical, Yao Wen-yuan—and 14 vice-chairmen, of whom Hsu Ching-hsien is one.

Although Hsu is among the 80 percent of the committee who are under 45, he spoke deprecatingly of his and his young colleagues' lack of experience. Of the total committee, 15 percent are military men (a high proportion), 15 percent are administrative staff, and 70 percent are "mass representatives," whom he enumerated as being workers, peasants, Red Guards, and intellectuals. It was the first time we had heard of Red Guards still being retained in an official post. Only 22 percent of the total number on the committee are women.

Hsu enumerated Shanghai's four major goals: (1) ideological education, by which he meant getting people to work without thought of personal gain; (2) speeding up industrial production without increasing pollution; (3) population control; and (4) medical treatment and public health.

It developed that what he was telling us when he used the words "ideological education" was that "sin" is not quite dead in Shanghai and that the government recognizes it has not totally tamed this once-wild city.

"We must make people aware that they are the true masters of their city," Hsu said in matter-of-fact tones. "There is still too much of the kind of thinking imposed by the imperialists and reactionaries who once ruled much of Shanghai," he explained. "Many capitalists remained after Liberation, and there are still people in Shanghai who have the idea that if a man doesn't work for personal gain, he stands to be condemned."

He said so many enterprises, or individual shops, were left over from the previous era that it was difficult to get people "to work for the revolution of the proletariat and socialist construction." Too often, he said, progress is interrupted by "bourgeois ideology."

"Ideological education will merely be suspended in midair if it is not accompanied by increased production to improve the conditions of the workers," Hsu said, in describing Shanghai's second goal. He stated candidly that the Chinese are well aware that they are way behind in the areas of automation and mechanization. He said they hoped to learn new techniques from other countries and they hoped to make a major effort to speed up their capability in assembly-line production methods.

He said Shanghai was determined not to make the mistake that other countries had made in laying waste the environment when they experienced an industrial revolution. "We are thinking about this problem day and night," he said, "because we can't develop industry at the expense of the health of the people."

Despite his brave words, Shanghai was under a blanket of smog most of the time we were there.

Nonetheless, Hsu told us of a recent campaign to eliminate some of the smoke from the 4,000 large smokestacks that serve Shanghai's 9,000 factories (not all of which emit harmful waste gases). Public opinion was mobilized against pollution, much as it has been in the United States (he called it "going to the masses"). As a result, devices to capture the waste gases have been installed on 50 percent of the offending smokestacks.

He told us that the cinders from the furnaces were being used to make bricks for the air-raid shelters that China continues to construct because of their suspicions of the Russians.

At this point, he digressed to tell us a fascinating story about how Shanghai had been sinking into the mud just as Chicago had in its early days.

In Hsu's terminology, the "imperialist capitalists" had used up so much water from the subterranean water table that the city sank by a full meter (about a yard). After city officials puzzled about this problem, according to Hsu, they thought of "going to the masses," who talked the problem over and suggested pumping water back into the ground, thus forcing the buildings of the city back up to their proper level.

The plan was adopted. Now, under water regulations in Shanghai, an industry must pay each year to have pumped back into the ground more water from the Whangpoo River than it uses. The pumping is carried out during the winter months, when water usage is light. Measurements indicate that, like Chicago in the 1850s, Shanghai is now rising out of its own muck at a rate of about 1 to 2 centimeters per year.

Population control, Hsu's third priority, was a subject we had discussed at many levels during our visit, mainly in terms of family planning. Much of the activity in this area—abortion, sterilization, and birth control through the pill and contraceptive devices—takes place at the clinics in the Communes and factories, and the experience of Shanghai is typical of the pattern.

With Liberation in 1949 and the sharp increase in the amount of food available, Shanghai experienced a soaring birth rate. In the early 1950s, the rate had reached 29 births per 1,000 population, or an annual gross increase of 290,000 people. This has been reduced to 7.5 births per 1,000 people in the city limits and a higher figure in the rural-suburban areas, for a net average of 12.5 births per 1,000 people. At a rate of 5 deaths per 1,000 people, the annual net growth was reduced to 75,000 per year.

Hsu deplored the old Chinese philosophy that "the more children you have, the happier you will be when you grow old." He called this an outgrowth of a feudal society, adding that "two children today is quite enough and three is a little bit too much." (Whether it is a coincidence or otherwise, almost every family we visited had three children.)

Though the deputy mayor did not discuss it, we learned from conversations at the various factories that the pill is the most popular form of birth control. Vasectomies are not popular with the men, but at one factory we learned that 30 of the 70 women in the plant had been sterilized through ligature of the Fallopian tubes. Abortions are performed on request, though not after three months of pregnancy.

Chiang Yun-hsiang is one of the chief administrative officers for the Tien Shan Workers Village, with a total population of 75,000.

It is unheard of for an unmarried person to ask for birth-control devices from a clinic, but they are for sale on the open market. Still, our hosts insisted that premarital sex before the age of 25 or 26 is almost nonexistent. It is fair to report that their American guests remained skeptical on this point, though perhaps the lack of privacy in this crowded land may prove deterrent enough.

Homosexuality is hardly in the vocabulary of most Chinese. When we asked the woman manager of a small factory about it, she had to have the word explained to her in Chinese. The interpreter finally hit upon "boy-boy" and "girl-girl" as the best explanation. To which the 45-year-old executive replied—to laughter in the room—"But how can that be?"

In the area of medical treatment, Shanghai's fourth goal, Hsu gave us another word picture of how revolutionaries are formed by recalling that, as a boy, he saw people kneeling at the pharmacy to beg for a penicillin shot for a sick relative. Now the cost of penicillin has been reduced to 20 to 30 Chinese fen (15¢), and medical care is either free at the factory or paid for with cheap medical insurance available in the Communes.

As in other large cities, Shanghai's government exists on many levels. One of the most fascinating of these is the Street Committee, or Neighborhood Committee—or as it is known only in Shanghai, the Lane Committee. These committees function as local administrative units, economic units, courts, security bureaus, and boards of education (they are responsible for the actual operation of the schools as well).

In Shanghai, we talked with Chiang Yun-hsiang, the vice-chairman of one of these committees. She is one of the chief administrative officers for Tien Shan Workers Village, where crane operator Lu Tsu-yung and his family live. She is a woman with a very expressive face, a quick mind, and an ability to field any questions tossed at her.

Tien Shan Workers Village was founded in 1952. Since then the city government has built 660 new apartment buildings in the area. There are 12 primary schools with 16,000 pupils; 6 middle schools with 8,400 pupils; and 12 nurseries and kindergartens with 2,000 children. Tien Shan has 2 hospitals and 13 clinics, with a total of 320 medical workers. The area has its own movie houses, an opera house, and a theater.

Also operated by the government, she told us, are 50 small production centers (craft shops) involved in making handicrafts (many of them for export) and providing needed municipal services. However, the fire and police departments are the responsibility of the city of Shanghai.

Security at Tien Shan is unobtrusive but effective. I was told, for example, that the lady I saw standing on the corner with an umbrella may well have been a Lane Committee member seeing that our visit went smoothly and that nothing happened to us.

When Ms. Chiang was asked the question about incorrigibility and the measures taken to integrate the individual into the social pattern, we were told that the Chinese resort to political education, repeated as often as necessary, in order to assure what they call "a correct line" in the person's thinking. (We would call it conformity.) At this point, she interjected a bit of dialectical jargon, saying that crime becomes a social contradiction and must be treated as such. Tien Shan Workers Village does not have a May 7 school or a farm of its own, but Ms. Chiang did not deny the possibility that if political education did not work, an individual might be sent to the countryside for manual labor and further "tempering."

The nurseries and kindergartens are really operated as day-care centers and as weekly boarding schools, with a completely fluid pattern as to which predominates. The day nurseries cost the worker 4 yuan per month; the boarding nursery, 5 yuan per month. The worker's factory contributes 2 yuan of this. At 18 months, babies are eligible to be enrolled in a housing-complex nursery. Before that, they may be kept in an infants' nursery at the factory where the mother is employed.

After our conference with Ms. Chiang, we visited two of the production centers. In one room, they were finishing handkerchiefs for export, and in another, they were producing embroidered brocade, also for export. The rooms were well-lighted and seemed to represent a modern Chinese version of cottage industries.

We went next to the market, which had a large variety of foods, including meat, fish, and poultry—a large wicker cage held about 25 live geese in it. As we stood there, a customer walked by with a live chicken in his hand. There was a special display counter for the different types of vegetables and also a counter for convenience foods—in this case Chinese dishes arranged artistically on a plate, all fresh, and which the individual could buy prepared for cooking when he or she returned from work. (Earlier, we had learned there were only 100,000 black-and-white TV sets in this land of 800 million people, so these convenience foods could not be called TV dinners.)

Visitors to the old Shanghai would no doubt find the Communist life-style dull. But it is obviously more important that today's Chinese find it comfortable.

12

Many Faces, One Voice

After several weeks in China, a visitor is left without any doubt that the government's program of indoctrinating everyone with a single point of view has been successful. In other totalitarian societies, speech reflects educational and cultural differences within the population, but in China speech varies only insignificantly. It makes no difference whether you are talking to a peasant, a worker, a university professor, or a plant manager; their responses to questions about their society and their role in it are identical in vocabulary as well as in viewpoint.

In a fearful parallel to the "newspeak" of George Orwell's novel of a totalitarian state, 1984, enemies of the state, such as Liu Shao-chi and Lin Piao, are referred to not by name, but by such terms as "other swindlers." When we asked the editors of the People's Daily why these men were not referred to by name, they replied placidly, "It is not necessary. Everyone knows whom we are talking about." Chou En-lai gave us the same answer.

As has been indicated, the indoctrination is persistent and continuous. Because much of it is conveyed to the provinces by telephone or radio and because printed materials are scarce, it is also possible to change the official line quite easily. Thus, after 20 years of propaganda attacking Americans as "running-dog imperialists" and other anti-American slogans, the "word" was suddenly passed that the Chinese were to be friendly to all "distinguished foreign visitors," including Americans and China's age-old invaders and persecutors, the Japanese.

The "word," of course, comes from Chairman Mao. Although we saw very few Little Red Books of *Quotations from Chairman Mao* other than in the bookstalls or on reading racks for foreigners, there was not a single interview in which replies to our most basic questions did not begin with a quote from the Chairman. It is an awesome experience to find that a culture and a nation (in China they are one and the same) can be totally permeated not only with a single belief, but with a common vocabulary.

Much of this propaganda effort is built upon the assumption of the perfectibility of human nature, a viewpoint reflected in their approach toward crime and the treatment of criminals.

In dealing with the question of law and order, the Western student of government will look in vain for the structure of public consensus that has evolved from our Greco-Roman heritage. The Chinese look rather to Confucius, whose point of view, as Lin Yutang once well described it, was "that politics must be subordinated to morals, that government is a makeshift of temporization, law a superficial instrument of order, and a police force a foolish invention for morally immature individuals."

John King Fairbank, the China expert, finds this reliance on the personal leader very much alive today. In his book *The United States and China* (Harvard University Press, 1971), Fairbank describes the Chinese view of the law in this way:

> In short, "the law" in China was an arm of the state and something to avoid—a very different institution from that which has nourished political leadership, guided legislation, trained statesmen, served corporations, and protected individual rights among the legal-minded and litigious American people.

Fairbank quotes Sun Yat-sen as once complaining that his people were like "a heap of loose sand." But rather than pack this sand into a mold, the Chinese prefer to leave it loose—relying, as Fairbank says, "upon ethics more than law, upon moral consensus more than judicial procedure."

As this is written, no Westerner—not even the late Edgar Snow—has been able to penetrate the veil of secrecy that shields the application of these principles to the enforcement of law and order in China today. The deputy mayor of Shanghai, Hsu Ching-hsien, was the first official who was willing to discuss in detail the current Chinese system of crime and punishment, but we were not allowed to see any part of the system in operation.

As might be expected, the worst crimes are considered to be political. In this totalitarian society, even with its use of what Chou En-lai called "ideological methods," opponents of the government are considered criminals, not dissenters.

Hsu described these and other offenders as the "bad elements," who have not been transformed by the Revolution and who cling to bourgeois thinking and habits. A second category of these "bad elements" was described as the troublemakers—the so-called new criminals who have been subject to "imperialist" or other evil social influences. The third category he mentioned was that of the few saboteurs or spies who have access to China, principally through Shanghai's seaport or airport.

He then mentioned specific crimes more common to Western society, predominantly graft, embezzlement, speculation, and theft. Hsu said they did not have many serious crimes and gave us the figures for August when, because of the warm weather and open doors and windows, crime is traditionally highest. In a city of almost 11 million people, he reported, there were only 63 criminal cases, and all were in the categories he mentioned. There were no crimes against persons.

The Chinese government today is philosophically dedicated to using political reeducation rather than confinement in dealing with all but the most serious criminals.

The system works as follows: If a person is accused of petty theft, for example, a meeting is held where he works, and he is "criticized" by his fellow workers in line with Mao's thinking. We would call it being held up to public ridicule by his peer group.

After such a discussion, a recommendation as to the punishment is made to "the courts." But we were never able to ascertain who runs the courts, how the judges are chosen, or even what relation the courts bear to the rest of the system.

If a crime is minor, the individual probably will be left on the job without special designation as a criminal, though it is self-evident that he will be under considerable surveillance. If it is a more serious crime of graft or embezzlement, prison sentences ranging up to 30 years may be imposed. Capital punishment is retained for the most serious crimes of rape, murder, counterrevolutionary activity, and sabotage.

We were told of one rape-murder case (the deputy mayor blamed pornographic literature left over from the old days) in which the masses demanded capital punishment. When one of our group asked the method employed, the deputy mayor replied somewhat tartly, in a manner showing that resentment toward the foreigner is not dead in Shanghai, "The firing squad, of course. What did you think we do?" he asked (figuratively drawing a knife across his throat). "Cut off their heads?"

The media and the arts also have roles to play in controlling the thoughts and actions of the people. Mao's methods, built as they are on pure doctrine rather than organizational control, call for both the reinforcement of belief through indoctrination and a constant testing of the state of the public mind.

In reply to a question from me, Chou En-lai described Mao's techniques as consisting of these steps (parenthetical phrases indicate how it might be expressed in non-Communist terminology):

1. Proceed from the facts (make an estimate of the situation).
2. All wisdom comes from the masses (check public opinion).
3. Concentrate the leadership in the masses (involve local grass-roots leaders).
4. Put it to the test of practice (try experimental programs under favorable conditions).
5. If it is proven, apply it in concentrated form.
6. Repeat Steps 1 through 5 as often as is necessary, going to and from the masses until the correct policy is formed.
7. Always integrate theory with practice.

The experience of the Communist Revolution in China shows how Mao applied these principles. Rather than trusting a central group of advisers to formulate party dogma, Mao first went into the countryside to find out what the peasants were willing to fight for (Steps 1 to 3). Then he put these goals in Communist Party terminology and played them back to the peasants (Steps 4 and 5). As events developed, he simply followed the principle of Step 6 to provide a level of support that would maintain his own power and satisfy the aspirations of the peasants, who were able to make a connection between Mao's dogma and the improvement of their own condition (Step 7).

The media are fundamental to this political process of maintaining a flow of communication between the leaders and the people, particularly as the people have no access to a ballot box to express their preferences. And the people are heard from. The *People's Daily* in Peking, the national newspaper of China, requires a staff of 30 people to handle the 500 letters to the editor received each day.

In China today, the editors do not consider it their duty to present the news in an impartial sense. Rather they take their direction from a speech that Mao made in 1948 to the staff of the provincial newspaper *Shansi Suiyuan Daily*. One sentence tells it all: "The role and power of the newspapers consist in their ability to bring the Party program, the Party line, the Party's general and specific policies, its tasks and methods of work before the masses in the quickest and most extensive way." At the *People's Daily*, the editors, who are called "leading members" of the newspaper's Revolutionary Committee, said they did not regard it as their duty to present the news, but rather to publicize the "correct line" of the government to the people.

Chu Mu-chih, the general director of Hsinhua, the official news agency, which gathers and dispenses all national and international news in China, put it more subtly. "We are keen on news that will explain the success of the social revolution and elucidate the policy of the Party and the revolutionary line of our Chairman," he said. He went on to say that every Chinese journalist adheres to a code of "fairness, accuracy, and responsibility" just as journalists in the United States do, but that code exists only within the framework of serving the Party and its goals.

The *People's Daily* has a circulation of more than 3 million and is distributed through the government post-office branches. It is not the biggest paper in China. In one of those marvelous Chinese circumlocutions, the government publishes a "private newspaper" with a digest of wire-service news from all over the world. This tabloid-sized paper—with a circulation of 6 million per day, or double that of the government's official national newspaper—is called *Reference News* or *For Reference Only*, depending on your preference in translation. As nearly as I could determine, it is distributed principally to local Party leaders or government officials.

Coexisting with these national publications are a series of provincial newspapers, some with a circulation of several hundred thousand. These provincial papers are among the most closely guarded secrets in China; we American editors were not allowed even to pick up a copy, let alone read it.

The Chinese were willing to describe the papers to us, however. They told us that the center two pages (most Chinese papers are only four pages) were devoted to letters from readers. Most of these letters criticized local officials, who the letter writers felt were not putting into practice what Mao expected of them. The most common complaints are about white-collar workers, or cadres, who seek to avoid manual labor.

From the descriptions of the papers and interviews with provincial editors, it appeared that these local dailies were being used as a sort of safety valve in the process of giving the masses a sense of participating in the development of government policy (Mao's Step No. 2). There is no human-interest news in these papers, and the headlines indicated that most of them dealt with increased agricultural output, industrial production, or labor heroes in action.

Augmenting these newspapers is one other national daily, *Kuang Ming*, which has a circulation of only 130,000, but goes to the intel-

Now-famous ballet *The Red Detachment of Women* dramatizes
battle of revolutionaries against landlords and their hired soldiers.

lectual leaders, scholars, and others concerned with ideology and forward opinion-making. It also reports on new trends in health and education.

The radio also plays an important role in this drumfire of ideological inundation. Propaganda newscasts, exhortations, and reports of socialist achievements are poured out against a background of martial music and stirring choruses of praise for Chairman Mao. Television is not yet an important news medium. The usual program begins and ends with a view of a proscenium arch and a curtain opening and closing, as if the viewer were watching a performance in a theater.

When the Chinese have a free evening to go to the theater, they get the same message they have already received from their radio, their newspaper, and the political class at their factory. Since the Cultural Revolution, no theater, ballet, or art is permitted unless it "serves the people" by promoting the purposes of the Communist regime. Even the great Peking Opera is now moribund, though its scenery is reported still intact so that performances could be resumed if any exceptions are eventually permitted to the insistence that all art serve the ends of propaganda.

Recently the Chinese have purchased rights to several American films, including the hit musical *The Sound of Music,* but it is not yet clear how wide the exposure of these films will be among the populace. Also the Chinese film makers are reported to be experimenting with nature documentaries in which the propaganda theme is at least muted and no longer central to the plot. But for the moment, most evenings in the theater consist of a program similar to this one I witnessed at the music hall in Sian:

SOIREE IN SIAN
October 1972

    I.   Folk Sings of Shensi-Kansu-Ningsia Border Region

   II.   Erh hu [two-stringed fiddle] Music:
        1. Up the Mountain Come the Manure Carriers
        2. Yangko Dance Hailing the Bumper Harvest

   III.   Dance: Weaving Fishnets

   IV.   Cittern Music:
        1. Happiness Channel
        2. Human Folk Song: Liu-yang River

   V.   Dance: There Is a Golden Sun in Peking

VI. Female Chorus:
   1. A Paean of Peking
   2. Tachai Yaksi (Fine Is Tachai)

VII. Dance: Picking Tea Leaves

VIII. Male Solo:
   1. We Poor People Follow Chairman Mao
   2. Great Peking

IX. Dance: Laundering Song

X. Flute Solo:
   1. Fine Is North Shensi
   2. Hearts of the Frontier Guards Turn to the Party

XI. Dance: Little Sisters on the Steppe

XII. Female Solo:
   1. Autumn Harvest (North Shensi Folk Song)
   2. Sing to Emancipation (North Shensi Folk Song)

+   +   +

Puppet Show

1. Sing to the PLA
2. Friendship Match
3. Instrumental Music

On another evening, I witnessed a performance of the famed *Red Detachment of Women* ballet. In the language of the program, it is the story of Wu Ching-hua, daughter of a poor peasant, who escapes the dungeon of despotic landlord Nan Pa-tien. She enlists in a Red Army unit, and "her class consciousness raised, makes up her mind to fight for the freedom of all mankind."

Finally, the Red Army liberates the slaves of Nan Pa-tien. "The despotic landlord is shot. The laboring people whose families have suffered for generations see the sun—revolutionary masses flock to join the Red Army. Battle songs resound to the skies." When the landlord is shot, the Chinese applaud with all the gusto of the audience at an early American melodrama, a word that accurately describes theater in China today.

Enigmatically, this emphasis upon art as propaganda is producing a wider participation in the arts than ever before. Formerly, there were only two national ballet companies and a few theater troupes, and these were for the elite in the major cities. Now, because every

Even ballet training has a propaganda theme.
This young dancer carries a spear in symbolic dance
that ends in defeat for "enemies of the state."

province has its own theater and dance school, the supply of trained talent in the performing arts is multiplying at a fantastic rate.

One of these schools I visited was the Shensi Song and Dance Ensemble and School in Sian. Here the emphasis on technique and discipline in the training of performers from 11 years of age on up was on a par with any professional training school in the world. Formerly called the Northwest Arts Troupe, the school moved to a campuslike series of buildings in Sian at the time of the Revolution and now consists of 430 full-time performers and 90 students.

Each art form—opera, song and dance, orchestra—and the student troupe have their own rehearsal halls and class facilities. The school also has its own Opera House, for which the top ticket price is 60¢. But much of the performing time is spent away from the school, providing entertainment at Communes, factories, and social clubs.

When asked about the effect of the Cultural Revolution on the school, the faculty told us that classes had been suspended for a year while most of the students participated in making "big-character" billboards promoting Mao's doctrines or in organizing Marxist study groups. They said some numbers were dropped from the repertoire because they were not "healthy"; that is, they did not advance the cause of the proletariat. The faculty members insisted, however, that only a small portion of their total repertoire was dropped.

Whether in the newspapers, in the slick paper periodicals, on the radio, or in the arts (all the emphasis is on performing arts, the plastic arts being pretty much restricted to traditional Chinese artifacts), the "line" is the same and the purpose is the same—*to serve the state.* There are no revolutionary poets, no underground novels, no minority or ethnic groups publicly expressing their restlessness, as in the Soviet Union.

This absence of dissent and the ability to achieve complete ideological control without the use of secret police—or, indeed, with only a minimum of uniformed police of any kind—are two of the most radical distinctions between China and the Soviet Union that are visible to a visitor who has traveled in both countries.

Chou En-lai told us this difference in atmosphere was due to the use of "ideological methods" rather than the "crude organizational methods" used by the Russians. Another reason may be that the Chinese Revolution is still a young revolution, one that has been able to concentrate on achieving limited goals and has not yet been faced with the problem of shifting to new goals after its initial objectives were achieved.

American pioneers, whether in the Puritan colonies of New England or on the western frontier, were able to insist on group loyalty and ban dissent because it could be shown that these principles were directly related to survival. China over the past two decades has been in much the same position. Millard Browne of the *Buffalo Evening News* described the atmosphere as being like that of a wartime economy, with self-sacrifice the watchword and ever-greater production the goal.

Certainly the Chinese people are much freer in speaking with you and in answering questions that in the Soviet Union would be considered hostile. However, it would be wrong to think that China feels totally secure about the support of its people. For example, there must be a reason that three hours or more per week in every factory or Commune is given over to political indoctrination. If the principles of Mao were truly as self-evident as we were told, would it then be necessary to continue these classes? Or as a member of a group of visiting Quakers put it in commenting on the new Chinese norms: "External pressures such as propaganda and group controls are still stressed and thus apparently still necessary."

Because China's Revolution is that of a single generation of leadership (the founders of the revolutionary movement half a century ago are still its leaders today), the question arises as to whether its commitment to self-sacrifice and lack of material motivation can be passed on to a second generation or to that majority of the population who are the youth of today and will be the great majority of the next decade. The youth of China have only secondhand knowledge of the "good old days," so the life that now seems so much better to their parents may not seem nearly good enough to them. American parents or grandparents who have tried to communicate the mood of the Depression years of the 1930s to today's affluent young people need no documentation of this problem.

Lord Macartney, the first British envoy to China, wrote in 1794 that "the common people of China are a strong, hardy race, patient, industrious and much given to traffic and all the arts of gain, cheerful and loquacious under the severest labor." His observations can be supported today, for we saw the Chinese people as cheerful, loquacious, and hardworking. But it should not be forgotten that Lord Macartney also described them as "much given to . . . all the arts of gain." It will be interesting to see how those arts are employed as China comes into contact with the commercial values of the outside world.

13

Changing China–
Some Final Impressions

ACKNOWLEDGMENT OF OUR IGNORANCE IS
THE NECESSARY BEGINNING OF WISDOM.
Chinese proverb quoted in *East Asian Civilization*

Impressions are really all the baggage a visitor can carry away after a relatively brief visit to the largest nation on earth—one that feeds, houses, and governs almost one-quarter of the world's people.

The first impression a cautious observer must mention, despite the echo-chamber quality of the Communist vocabulary to which he has been subjected, is that China is changing rapidly. Many times, I found that policies had been changed in the last three months, six months, or year as China "settled down" to a pragmatic compromise with the Cultural Revolution that had altered the Chinese social structure between 1966 and 1970.

Moderates are in fashion again, and ultraleftists (the Chinese term) are out of fashion. Even as we were leaving China, a letter that Chairman Mao supposedly wrote his wife, Chiang-ching, in July of 1966 deploring the Mao cult of personality, mysteriously began being distributed within China. The letter is filled with Mao aphorisms, and experts say it is written in his style, whatever the date.

It is also worth noting that in the letter he blames Lin Piao (disgraced Number 2 man in China, killed in a plane crash trying to flee) with promoting the cult of the Little Red Books. Mao, in a public act of personal disavowal, wrote, "I have never believed those few booklets of mine possess so much fantastic magic. Now, thanks to his [Lin Piao's] propaganda, the whole nation has been aroused."

The disclosure of the letter is also an indication of Mao's astute sense of political timing. It did not appear until after the Little Red Books had completely vanished from the hands of every Chinese in an early demonstration of total control. The change was dramatic: A French film maker was showing hundreds of feet of film of Chinese waving Little Red Books of *Quotations from Chairman Mao* taken only six months before my visit, yet in my travels of thousands of miles, I did not see a single person waving a Little Red Book.

In his letter, Mao hardly takes himself off the stage. "Where there is no tiger," he writes in another part of the letter, "the monkey becomes king of the mountain." This epigram of Mao's is a reminder to Western observers that the Chinese have never accepted the Aristotelian dictum that a government of laws is better than a government of men. Consequently, Mao, through personal leadership and dominance, has been able to raise the art of political management to its most efficient level for the short term. However, he has left his loyal followers in China without answers to some long-term questions that cannot be evaded.

The first of these is the succession of leadership to Mao himself. If, in the mid-1970s, Mao will not or cannot fill all the places on the ruling Politburo—because he still feels insecure—or if he will not or dare not publicly identify a second level of leadership, which may be considered in training for succession to power, then the Chinese ship of state must inevitably rock in turbulent waters when his controlling hand is either enfeebled or removed.

This prospect of a disruptive period after Mao's death does not necessarily perturb the Chinese as much as it does those of us in the Western democracies who regard stability as a fundamental virtue of government and who are accustomed to an orderly transition of power. Hegel's philosophy of "thesis-antithesis-synthesis" by which change is assumed to occur has been translated by Mao into the current Communist doctrine of "struggle-criticism-transformation." Mao's peculiarly Chinese interpretation of this philosophy assumes that some of this change will be revolutionary in character.

Although China has had a single administration in power for 24 years, it has undergone, within the past 15 years, two turbulent periods, which have literally rocked the nation. When Mao attempted to stimulate the economy with the Great Leap Forward in 1958, it required more than two years to get the country back to where it had been before he started his campaign to have peasants operate backyard steel furnaces and other improbable industrial enterprises. When Mao launched the Cultural Revolution, its excesses brought many normal governmental activities and all of higher education to a dead halt for almost four years.

Listen to 26-year-old Soong Wen-hua of Canton as he looks ahead to the future and shows the effects of the indoctrination he has been receiving. "We have gone through several critical periods since we began the Revolution in the 1920s," he says, "*and we expect more to come.* [Italics mine] People don't want their normal lives disturbed, but you just can't avoid it. In seven or eight years, we will have another period of upheaval. But because of these periods, we are moving the people from a lower state of class consciousness to a higher state. Theoretically, our new leaders will emerge from this class struggle."

In other words, whoever wants the brass ring after Mao's demise is going to have to grab it himself. No maker of a revolution has ever successfully designated his own heir, and it is the view of China expert Owen Lattimore that Mao is too wise to try. Nor is there any reason to believe that any new leadership structure will be able to wield the same kind of power that flowed from Mao's personal dynamism or will have his ability to articulate goals for China's common man.

Because respect for one's elders is a Chinese tradition undiminished by either Communist doctrine or the Cultural Revolution, one can forecast that whatever leader or leaders do emerge to replace Mao and Chou will have been "tempered" by Party leadership and Party training. As Chou said, they will not be young enough to be inexperienced (as he said he had been in the 1920s), but they will be mature enough to fit naturally into the structure and tradition that brought them to power.

Mao's Revolution has other problems. One of them is technology. An example of China's backwardness in this area is the fact that even in 1900 under the feudal government of the czars, Russia already had a higher per capita production of pig iron, steel, and cotton goods and more railroad track per square mile than China had more than half a century later.

Fairbank has pointed out that the current backwardness in technology is by no means a necessary heritage of Chinese culture. Until late medieval times, China actually led the way in technological inventiveness and scientific observation of the universe. China developed paper and printing; chemical explosives; the mechanical clock (I saw one clock in the Forbidden City run by dripping water); cartography; the beginnings of pharmacology; the principles of the compass, the crossbow, and the kite; and even the principle by which today we translate the vertical motion of the piston into lateral locomotion for our automobiles.

Whether it was the decay or corruption of the Chinese Imperial

China still moves by manpower and not by machines, as this picture
of a city roadway dramatically illustrates.

Court or the disruption caused by the invasion of foreign powers that halted these developments in the field of science and technology has been the subject of much debate and few conclusions. But it is indisputable that throughout the first half of the 20th century, China lagged even further behind the West in these areas.

The leaders of the new China have given the country a new set of priorities geared to the demands of this modern world. The priorities of China today, I was told over and over again, are first, agriculture; second, light industry; and third, heavy industry. Or as Chou put it, "Agriculture is our first priority, with light industry a leading factor."

There is no doubt that China has achieved her first priority. The Chinese people are fed, and in many areas, are storing grain against lean years.

The question now becomes one of the second priority, or Chou's "leading factor." Can Mao find the techniques necessary to motivate and train the industrialized and skilled workers who must make these new priorities effective?

Throughout his revolutionary career, Mao has shown greater aptitude in providing leadership for rural peasants than for the workers in the cities, with their more complex relationships and problems. For example, in the 1920s, Mao found he could not sell his credo to the urban proletariat and was forced to rest his power base on an agrarian revolution.

Indisputably, the time is at hand when China's agrarian culture must come face-to-face with a modern oriental updating of the Industrial Revolution. New machinery, new trade contracts, and new exchanges of journalists, doctors, and technicians mean an infusion of new ideas into a society isolated for more than two decades.

The question is not whether this will occur, but rather how China will attempt to handle and control these new forces. An administrative bureaucracy for planning, cost control, and distribution is an inescapable by-product of mechanization and mass production. Fortunately for the Chinese, they seem to have emphasized the principle of decentralization to a degree that will enable them to avoid the cumbersome centralized bureaucracy of the Russian model.

It is also clear that a modification of the present system of rewards is inevitable as consumer goods become available. Historically, total egalitarianism based on self-sacrifice has only been possible when there is nothing to distribute. Even in China today, as Warren Phillips of the *Wall Street Journal* observed, "Material incentives are widely denounced and just as widely employed." The tractor driver, for instance, earns more than the field hand; the technically trained worker earns more than the unskilled worker. It is only a step from a position as an official of a Revolutionary Committee to membership in the managerial class.

Dissent in the Soviet Union did not surface until there was a wide awareness of the possibility of acquiring consumer items related to greater personal comfort and leisure-time enjoyment. The same is likely to be true in China. One can imagine, for example, that when the first ten commuters in Peking acquire cheap Japanese motors to run their bikes, the other 1,699,990 bike owners who see these motorized cyclists are likely to discover that something is missing in their lives.

Mao appears to have little use for education as an end in itself or for the pure research that must precede technical innovations and the introduction of new technology. There is only the scantiest evidence that Mao is prepared to deal with this problem, though it is quite clear to an outsider that it requires more than "a high level of political consciousness" to build an automated factory or program a computer.

There is some evidence that government at a lower level is attempting to evade the excesses of dogma engendered by the Cultural Revolution and make it possible for China to speed up the training of much-needed specialists and engineers. One recent report from Hsinhua, the official news agency, indicates that only half the usual number of young people are being sent down to the countryside this year. Other reports, though less official, indicate that a small number of middle-school graduates with special aptitudes are again being allowed to go directly into universities and technical schools for special training.

There can only be one explanation for this deviation from the dogmatic practice of requiring every middle-school graduate to spend up to two years in rural areas. The needs have become so great that dogma must be set aside, or if past experience means anything, a new dogma will be developed to meet this new situation.

The question of China's relationships with her neighbors, principally the Soviet Union, also enters into the equation. Napoleon once said, "Let China sleep, for when she wakes, the whole world will tremble." Anyone who has read these pages or the newspapers of the past two years will agree that China is indeed awake and proud of her own competence and destiny.

China will "continue to follow faithfully the proletarian world revolutionary line in world affairs," Chou En-lai told us. But when

Fear of an attack by the Soviet Union has led to continued emphasis on guerrilla warfare and the training of local militia, such as this group of part-time soldiers at Yenan.

an editor suggested that this meant China was thinking of moving outward, Chou answered with a rhetorical question, "How could a socialist state expand outward? Our system itself would not permit that. We have lots more land to work and the population to work it. . . ."

China's current military posture is unquestionably oriented chiefly to defense—particularly against a possible nuclear strike from the Soviet Union. We saw many soldiers in China, but very few with guns; most were workers or farmers. We did see an airfield with a flotilla of huge troop-carrying helicopters, MIG fighters lined up in dress formation on a civilian airport runway, and submarines and small rocket-launching torpedo boats in the Whangpoo River. In Yenan, we saw guerrilla fighters in training; China still considers them its last line of defense.

With millions of troops on either side of the Sino-Soviet border, there is certainly no reason to expect any lessening of tension between these two nations within the foreseeable future. Nor should the possibility of the massive movement of troops across the border be ruled out. But it is extremely difficult to believe the Chinese view that they live in fear of a nuclear strike by the Soviet Union. The Russians, after all, have their own problems; the pressure for consumer goods in the Soviet Union, which allocates a major portion of its budget to armaments, is much greater than the comparable pressure in China.

Another factor that must have a deterrent effect on the Russians is that the weapons gap between the two nations is not nearly so great as it was a decade ago. Like the Soviet Union, China seems to have been able to draw from its best minds and best scientists and assign them effectively to the creation of a special technology—that of producing nuclear warheads and missiles. The Russians showed this could be done when they startled the world with Sputnik. In China, a comparable effort, with highly concentrated priorities, has resulted in the creation of a nuclear arsenal, which the U.S. government estimates may be as high as four dozen missiles in well-protected locations, all with hydrogen-bomb warheads and all with the capability of reaching targets deep in the Soviet Union.

Finally, it is necessary to keep in mind that aggression has many faces and names. A nation committed to "proletarian world revolution" may not consider it aggression to export that revolution. Chinese philosophers have contributed to this view since ancient times. The *Book of Tao*, for example, contains what Lin Yutang called the first enunciated philosophy of camouflage in the world: "It teaches the wisdom of appearing foolish, the success of appearing to fail, the strength of weakness, and the advantage of lying low, the benefit of yielding to your adversary, and the futility of contention for power." Two centuries later, Chinese generals were already learning from a military classic, the *Sun-tzu,* that "the acme of skill in warfare is to subdue the enemy without fighting."

In *The Long Revolution* (New York: Random House, 1972), the late Edgar Snow, a close friend of Mao Tse-tung and Chou En-lai and a sympathetic interpreter of China to the West, left his own warning about relations with China:

> The millennium seems distant and the immediate prospect is for the toughest kind of adjustment and struggle. China must satisfy Korea and Vietnam and the U.S. cannot jettison Japan. The danger is that Americans may imagine that the Chinese are giving up communism—and Mao's world view—to become nice agrarian democrats. A more realistic world is indeed in sight. But popular illusions that it will consist of a sweet mix of ideologies, or an end to China's faith in revolutionary means, could only serve to deepen the abyss again when disillusionment occurs. A world without change by revolutions— a world in which China's closest friends would not be revolutionary states—is inconceivable to Peking. But a world of relative peace between states is as necessary to China as to America. To hope for more is to court disenchantment.

With the end of the Vietnam war and the movement toward normalization of relationships with the United States, much of the previous tension and pressure from outside China has been reduced or eliminated. This opening of the doors is one of the factors that will make a transition to a modern economy much easier than would have been the case before. Certainly the United States, still smarting from Vietnam, is not likely to try to attach any political strings to economic or technological aid that might be offered to China in an effort to open up that vast market.

From these observations, I think it can be seen that the pressure for modernization from within and the fear of retribution from their former Communist partner the Soviet Union from without are the principal factors being weighed by the government leaders in Peking. How well these pressures can be balanced out or reduced is likely to determine whether the successes of the past 24 years can be duplicated or exceeded in the years to come.

While their leaders wrestle with these larger problems, the Chinese people themselves maintain a disarming air of friendliness and equanimity. The mental attitude of the people is best reflected in the smiles that seem to lie right at the surface of 90 percent of those you see or pass in the streets. A wave from a car, a nod, or a quick *Knee how* ("How are you?") produces an instant smile, even from workers bent over their hoes in the fields.

One final anecdote will serve to illustrate many points—the quality of life in China today, the friendliness to foreigners, and the extraordinary ability to project a single point of view to every layer of society.

On the last night of our trip, we gave a dinner for the escorts and interpreters who had accompanied us throughout our three-week visit. In the course of the toasts, we brought out the cooks and the waiters and waitresses to salute them not only for that night but as representatives of those responsible for all the exquisite food and excellent service we had received throughout our stay.

The responses from a cook and waitress were brief, articulate, and right out of the Mao manual. They apologized for not doing better, asked for our criticism, and assured us they were trying to improve. These self-effacing comments came after we had been served a 10-course dinner of approximately 18 dishes, with fresh salad served in sculpted melons. Each table had a centerpiece of chrysanthemums and roses carved from vegetables by a culinary artist.

The waitress was shy in responding to our applause. But when she did speak, her words were an echo of those of the premier of China:

"We know we have not done well," she said, modestly avoiding our accolades, "but we are a developing country, and we must try to do better."

The key word is "developing," for that is China's goal and that is the excitement of a journey to China. The country is changing. Change is inherent in its structure; it is foreshadowed by the age of its leaders; and it is implicit in the need for the Revolution to create new goals and new motivations.

China will never be "old China" again.

Appendix

TIPS FOR TOURISTS

No one can predict when the doors will be open to tourism. The Chinese officials with whom I spoke during my visit refused even to speculate on the time span needed to make preparations for general tourism in China. They simply smile and say, "We cannot tell at this time, but we are not keen on such groups now."

The reasons for this reluctance are twofold. First and primary is the absence of an adequate supply of English-language translators, even though English is now the second language in the schools. But the effects of 24 years of isolation, with little chance to speak the language, will not be quickly overcome.

The second reason is the shortage of what might be called traditional tourist points of interest and activities. A visitor might be kept busy for as much as a week in Peking, but even in this city of over 7½ million, there are few opportunities for evening entertainment.

A third shortage is that of automobiles. We did see some modern tourist buses, but the demands for public transportation in a nation where even a bicycle is still a luxury leaves little margin to provide wheels for tourism.

Sooner or later, of course, the gates will inevitably open.

At the present time, the People's Republic of China is a country without an up-to-date English-language guidebook, and it is likely to remain that way for some time. Observations based on my personal experiences may therefore be helpful to anyone who has hopes of being among the few thousand Americans now being admitted each year.

HOTELS

You will not be able to choose your hotel in China; it will be assigned to you by the China Travel Service. But no matter where you stay, it won't hurt your pocketbook. In checking up, I found that our cost per person averaged $23 a day, which included the hotel, food, and a chauffeur-driven private car. Prices have since been increased but are still below most other countries.

Your room will be large, furnished with 19th-century-style furniture, drab, and—with the exception of the bathroom floor—clean. Why the Chinese can keep the rest of the hotel clean and leave the white tile of the bathroom floor covered with a dusty clay film escaped me; but they have compensated by providing two pairs of immaculately clean rubber clogs in every room so that you don't have to step on the floor.

There is a room boy on every floor, but unless you speak a little Chinese or he is learning English (many are), the chances of getting room service without an interpreter are slim. Don't pay any attention to the call buttons in your room or the electric boxes on the wall over the floor stations; they were disconnected years ago.

Anyone who has been in a Russian hotel will find the appointments comparable, including the plumbing and the dim light over the sink. Usually Western guests will find a roll of Western-style toilet paper in the bathroom, but it is not a bad idea to carry a personal supply in the event the floor boy has a lapse of memory.

Hotel lobbies are unlike any you have seen. There are no registration desks, as you will have been registered when the China Travel Service assigned you to the hotel. A small information desk, a refreshment stand (sometimes with fresh fruit and groceries), a desk for mailing your postcards and letters, and a counter for changing money complete the amenities. Inquiry may also reveal a barbershop around the corner, where you can get a haircut (close to the head) and a shampoo for 30¢.

One of the pleasant customs of the hotels is that of leaving a canister of hot water outside your door each morning so you may have a cup of tea to start the day.

Hot water to wash in is less dependable; in rural areas, it may not exist at all or for only an hour or two a day. Plumbing can be erratic; at one hotel, there was no hot water from the faucet in the sink but plenty from the faucet in the bathtub. In Sian, a city of more than a million, hot water for washing and shaving was available in the hotel only between 7:00 and 9:00 a.m. and 7:00 and 9:00 p.m. each day.

The Chinese like their beds hard, and usually we slept on a thin mattress resting on a board. Bed linen is of plain white cotton, not ironed, but it seemed to be clean. A sheet is provided over the mattress, and the customary comforter is encased in a top mattress cover, also of cotton. The comforter is your top sheet. The bed usually has two small pillows with a small rough towel on the top; the towel is not for drying your hands but is the equivalent of our pillowcase and should be left in place.

One other item about towels in public places. You will find they are as wet as a washcloth. This is not because they have been used; China is a hot country for the most part, and the Chinese keep the towels wet because it is considered more refreshing.

MONEY

American Express checks are accepted in all the major cities. The basic Chinese currency consists of these units: a yuan (Chinese dollar—worth 43¢), a chiao (their 10¢ piece), and a fen (pronounced "fun"—their penny). The currency comes in units of 1 yuan, 2 yuan, 5 yuan, and 10 yuan, with nothing larger than 10 yuan. The smallest paper money is 1 chiao. The coins come in 5 fen, 2 fen, and 1 fen.

You cannot take money out of the country, but on the train going from Canton to the border town of Shumchun, an accommodating banker changes your Chinese currency to Hong Kong dollars.

FOOD

The food at the hotels is exquisite and an experience in itself. We were served a minimum of 6 dishes at every meal and sometimes as many as 18. Every meal was accompanied by a delicious soup.

American-style breakfasts of fried eggs or oatmeal are available in all major cities, and even coffee is easy to come by. However, the coffee addict would be wise to take his own instant coffee with him as coffee is usually available only at breakfast.

It was our observation that large groups of travelers, such as we American editors or a Peruvian Ping-Pong team, tended to eat better than smaller groups of three or four around the dining room. This is because of the nature of Chinese cuisine, in which the fish, chicken, or duck is traditionally put on the table whole.

CLIMATE

China in the summertime is one of the hottest places in the world, and there is no air-conditioning.

The climate in southern China is comparable to Hong Kong's.

Temperatures are in the 70s in the wintertime and in the high 80s in the summer.

During the winter, the average low at Peking is 25° F., while the average high is 32° F. However, the temperature frequently drops to zero. There is little precipitation in the north, but it increases as one moves south. At Shanghai, the average winter temperature is 38° F., 43° F. at Hangchow, and 56° F. at Canton.

In Peking and elsewhere in northern China, the fall and spring weather can be very unreliable, almost dangerous, shifting from hot to bone-chilling cold almost overnight. Anytime after mid-September, sweaters and warm clothing should be taken.

CLOTHING

Chinese men do not wear Western-style coats or ties, but they will expect visitors to do so at banquets, or "formal" dinners. Otherwise dress is very casual, with sport shirts a natural and accepted costume.

For women, pants suits are acceptable for all occasions as well as being ideal for travel. A cocktail dress may be worn for evening affairs, but fancy jewelry or beaded dresses will not be looked on with favor. And miniskirts are to be packed at the Hong Kong border and not taken out until your return.

TELEPHONE

Because of the language barrier, you are not likely to use the telephone much within China. A local telephone directory, even if available, would be unreadable to a Westerner.

Calls to the United States from the principal cities are relatively simple to make. The connections are good, and the conversation is easy to hear and understand.

The usual procedure is to ask at the hotel desk for a form that you can fill out in English. It requires your name and the name, area code, and telephone number of the person you are calling in the United States. Within a few minutes, an English-language operator will call you (from either the hotel or the overseas switchboard in Shanghai), telling you when you may expect your call to be completed.

Unless you have a card permitting collect calls to certain designated numbers in the United States, you will have to pay cash for the call when it is completed. Charges run about $50 for a three-minute call from Shanghai or Peking to the United States.

WATER

In your room, there is usually a carafe of water, which may have been filled from the tap. Halazone tablets are recommended, although in the major cities, the water is usually safe.

The Chinese themselves drink only boiled water, either straight or in the form of tea, and it is suggested that visitors do likewise. The water served in hotels has been boiled, and mineral water and soda water are available.

LAUNDRY

The laundry service is excellent. Neatly pressed clothes, with an identification tag sewn in, come back the same day. The little dry cleaning we required was performed just as quickly.

ELECTRIC RAZORS

Electric current is 220 volt, and a transformer is a necessity. Wall sockets do not take either European or American plugs, so an adapter is necessary. Room attendants in large hotels usually have an adapter you can borrow; however, it does not change current, so you will always need a transformer.

TIPPING

There is absolutely no tipping. It is considered an insult if you offer a tip.

SHOPPING

There is no bargaining. Prices are fixed by the state.

PERSONAL GIFTS

Chinese will accept "friendship gifts" if given on a proper occasion. They like books about the United States (with pictures), but such gifts as transistor radios are taboo.

CAMERAS

You cannot take pictures from the air, but you can take them just about any place else. The Chinese don't like it if you are obvious about photographing some of their poorer areas. Individuals are usually cooperative about having their pictures taken, but it's wise to have the interpreter ask for permission first.

FILM

The color film you have in China is the film you take in. Except for some British 35-mm black-and-white film, we found no Western color film on sale.

CIGARETTES

You are never out of reach of a cigarette in China—if you like Chinese cigarettes.

LIQUOR

The Chinese have no cocktail hour. If you must have your scotch or gin, take a bottle with you. There is a Chinese vodka, but it is raw. Americans desperate for a predinner cocktail might try the brandy on sale at the hotel refreshment counter; it mixes well with water.

ANTIQUES

We found only three shops left in Peking's Liu Li Chang, the traditional street of antique shops, and very little to buy except for temple rubbings and knickknacks. For purchases of large items, an additional obstacle is that it is difficult to have anything shipped out of the country. For a tourist with limited time, it is strictly cash and carry.

A small red-wax seal, or "chop," attached to an article means the government certifies it as a true antique. But with some minor exceptions, nothing more than 80 years old can be taken out of the country.

Some antique shops will make you a "chop," or sealing stamp, with the Chinese version of your name on it. A good souvenir.

TRANSPORT

The trains are modern, they run on time, and the engineers so skillful you cannot tell whether you are riding behind a steam engine or a diesel.

Air travel is very little used, and the flights are so infrequently scheduled that they constitute a barrier to tourist travel. For example, some cities of medium size are served by air only twice a week.

THEATER

Such theater as there is consists of morality plays and dances extolling the glories of Mao Tse-tung and his unique articulation of Communist philosophy. Even though most Americans won't be able to understand anything more than an oft-repeated *Mao chew see* (Chairman Mao), it is really rather pleasant to watch and for the most part professionally done.

Traditional Chinese music and instruments are still heard, but the Peking Opera is dead, or at least moribund. Unless there is an abrupt change, the average tourist would be well-advised to bring plenty of books to read and playing cards with a long life expectancy.

HOSPITALITY

Today, the friendliness of the people to foreigners is extraordinary and obviously a matter of policy as well as basic human nature. You also will be walking the safest streets in the world.

Some of our Chinese hosts told me that one of the reasons for approaching tourism slowly is that they wish "to be able to take care of our guests." And indeed they seemed to take the matter of our personal well-being as their direct responsibility. Members of our group who went out alone sometimes had the feeling they were being followed, but there was no interference with picture taking or any other activity; the Chinese just seemed determined to prevent the occurrence of any untoward incident.

LANGUAGE

Except at the front desk of your hotel or at the Friendship Stores —which sell only to foreigners—you are not likely to find many people who speak English. Thus, while you are theoretically free to go anywhere you want, it is not easy because of the language barrier.

You can buy most things by pointing or by pulling out your Chinese currency, but outside of the Friendship Stores, you are not likely to find consumer items that would appeal to you. So you can scratch shopping as an activity that will eat up any considerable amount of time.

VACCINATIONS

An international certificate of smallpox vaccination less than three years old is required to enter China. People leaving China by way of Hong Kong need a cholera vaccination less than six months old to enter the colony.

CUSTOMS REGULATIONS

Chinese customs authorities allow a limited quantity (corresponding to "what may reasonably be consumed by one person") of cigarettes, tobacco, and alcohol to be brought into the country, although no official document exists confirming this. About 200 cigarettes and two or three bottles of spirits seem to be the allowance for each person. You must declare electronic gadgets, jewelry, and watches on your customs declaration going in and account for them coming out.

MEDICINES

Pharmacies in major cities have a wide variety of high-quality medicines, including many modern antibiotics. However, because instructions are in Chinese, it would be better for the visitor to bring a supply of commonly needed medicines, such as Lomotil, Coricidin, and aspirin.

TIME

Peking time applies to the whole country. It is 13 hours ahead of Eastern Standard Time. When it is midnight in Washington, D.C., it is 1:00 p.m. in Peking; 6:00 p.m. in Washington is 7:00 a.m. in Peking.

TAXIS

Taxis must be called by telephone. Taxi prices are fixed. Only one passenger is allowed to ride in the front with the driver. Except in Peking, pedicabs are often available and inexpensive. The charge is about 20¢ per kilometer, or .62 mile. It is slightly higher at night and in poor weather.

RECOMMENDED FOR TOURISTS

Among the places we visited which I believe will be of special interest to American tourists are the following:

PEKING

Peking is the capital of the People's Republic of China. It is the traditional seat of government and today has a population of 7,570,000.

At the center of the city are majestic Tien An Men (Gate of Heavenly Peace) and Tien An Men Square. The square is the focus of all major celebrations and parades, which explains the permanent reviewing stands. At the south of the square is the Monument to the People's Heroes. On the west is the Great Hall of the People, where President Nixon met with Chou En-lai and where state banquets are held. On the east, housed in one building, are the Museum of the Chinese Revolution and the Museum of Chinese History.

The Palace Museum (formerly the Forbidden City) is the former palace of the emperors and empresses of the Ming Dynasty (1368–1644) and Ch'ing Dynasty (1644–1912). It is the largest and most complete existing ensemble of traditional Chinese architecture in the world, as well as an expression of complete artistic symmetry. The buildings, some of them more than 550 years old, cover almost 180 acres; there are more than 9,000 individual rooms, where the emperors lived and carried on the principal business of government.

More about these dramatic buildings may be found in Fodor's *Peking* or in a small pamphlet "The Former Imperial Palaces," published in English by the Chinese government. Allow a day or possibly more for the tour of these magnificent buildings and grounds. Because guides are sensitive about the extravagance of these courts and do not volunteer much information, you will be wise to carry your own reference book with you.

Pei-hai Park, just north of the Palace Museum, is beautifully situated on a large lake. It's a good place to watch the Chinese taking their ease.

The Temple of Heaven, some distance southwest from the Forbidden City, was the place where the Ming and Ch'ing emperors made their own kowtows and offered sacrifices and prayers for a propitious year. Fodor judges it to be the most famous temple in China and one of the wonders of the world.

The Summer Palace, at the northwest outskirts of the city, was an imperial garden in the 12th century. During the Ch'ing Dynasty, foreign troops ransacked and destroyed the grounds, which had been beautifully maintained for 700 years. Then in the 1850s, Empress Tzu-hsi diverted money appropriated for building up the navy to restore the Summer Palace. The only boat she built was one of marble, with curved bow and stone paddle wheels, which now sits placidly on Kun-ming Lake.

The Peking Zoo, the country's largest, is the home of the musk oxen that President Nixon gave China as a gift from the American people. But those who visit the zoo will not find any sign (or at least they didn't in October of 1972) telling zoo visitors the significance of the presence of the musk oxen.

The Ming Tombs and the Great Wall. These two tourist attractions combine to make an interesting day's tour from Peking. The approach to the 13 Ming tombs is lined with stone statuary of a variety of animals, both real and legendary. The tomb (Chang Ling) of Emperor Yunglo (1403–24) and the Underground Palace (Ting Ling) of Emperor Wan Li (1573–1620) are the two principal attractions.

The section of the Great Wall that has been restored and is customarily visited is at Pa-Ta-Ling. It is a steep climb to the upper reaches of the restored section and not to be recommended for anyone with cardiac difficulties. There is often a strong gale, so only the foolhardy will leave their warm clothes behind in Peking.

HANGCHOW

Hangchow has always been one of the principal tourist centers for the Chinese, and it is certain to be as popular with Americans and other foreign visitors. Views of the city's picturesque stone bridges and traditional Chinese palaces were among the visual highlights of the television coverage of President Nixon's visit to China.

Hangchow is the capital of Chekiang Province and is located on a bay about 100 miles southwest of Shanghai. The city's famous West Lake is a tourist mecca. Here flat-bottomed scows allow the visitor to drift dreamily over the surface of the water. Along the shore and on four small islands in the lake are many gardens, statues, and temples.

Marco Polo, who passed through Hangchow on his famous expedition in the thirteenth century, described it as "the greatest city which may be found in the world, where so many pleasures may be found that one fancies himself to be in paradise."

Stone statues guard imperial roadway leading to Ming Tombs in hills near Peking.

SIAN

Sian, once the ancient capital of the Han Empire, is now a flourishing textile center. The Sian Bell Tower is an ancient landmark and interesting example of restored Chinese architecture.

The Panpo Museum is a unique archaeological museum, as the Chinese have literally built a roof over the remains of a 6,000-year-old matriarchal village in order to preserve it and make it accessible to visitors. The prehistoric Panpo Village was discovered in 1953 on the east bank of the Chan River; the museum was opened in 1958.

Huaching Hot Spring. These mineral hot baths are 15 miles east of Sian at the foot of Lishan Hill in the Tsinling Mountains. This is a beautiful spot where emperors took their ease and where one of them, Hsuan Tsung of the T'ang Dynasty, carried on a famous love affair with his son's wife, a young beauty named Yang Kuei-fei. Their story is often celebrated in Chinese literature. This is also the spot from which Chiang Kai-shek was kidnapped by a Manchurian warlord in 1936 and then ransomed (to their later regret) in negotiations with a Communist group under the leadership of a young revolutionary with a black beard named Chou En-lai.

These hot springs, with a constant temperature of 110° F. and containing, according to the Chinese, at least nine minerals, are certainly worth a visit—and a bath.

YENAN

Yenan, a city of 70,000, somewhat isolated in the sandy mountains of Shensi Province, has been well-described as the Valley Forge of the Chinese Revolution. It was here that the surviving elements of Mao's Red Army established their base in 1936 after an 8,000-mile forced march of more than a year from southern bases in Fukien and Kiangsi provinces.

Yenan is also interesting for its many cave dwellings, ranging in ornateness from simple holes dug into the clay hills to stone houses with traditional wood and paper Chinese entryways. Tourist accommodations are good but limited in number (a 60-room guest house). Access is either by a long bus ride or infrequently scheduled planes (the airport consists of a single runway made of square cobblestones).

The tours of Yenan will take you to the four places where Mao stayed during the time he was in Yenan, as well as to the site of the Seventh Party Congress in 1945.

Yenan's role in modern Chinese history is emphasized by the paintings and photographs of its famous bridge and pagoda, which may be found in almost every public building in China.

Yenan has been scarred many times. In 1939, it was bombed by the Japanese and destroyed. Much of it was bombed or shelled in 1947 by Chiang Kai-shek's Kuomintang armies. It was during these last attacks that the famous pagoda was destroyed; the Communists carefully restored it during the 1950s, though it has no religious significance.

CANTON

Canton is already the most familiar city in China to Americans because of the famous Canton Trade Fair, or as they call it, The Chinese Export Commodities Fair, held in the spring and fall. In one building, a visitor can see commodities from every area of China and gain a real measure of the ability of the country to produce food and to manufacture consumer goods and industrial products.

RECOMMENDED REFERENCES FOR TOURISTS

Fodor's *Peking* by Odile Cail (McKay)
   Excellent guide and history, with interesting walking tours. Some information on shops and restaurants outdated slightly as Chinese continue to change the system.
Illustrated Atlas of China (Rand McNally)
   Up-to-date information on country's resources, industry, agriculture, and climate. Magnificent maps.
Tourist Map of Peking (Foreign Language Press, Peking)

IMPORTANT DATES IN CHINESE HISTORY

The Imperial Period

c. 1767–1123 B.C.	*Shang Dynasty*	Bronze Age
c. 1124–256 B.C.	*Chou Dynasty*	Feudalism established (Confucius c. 551–478 B.C.)
221–206 B.C.	*Ch'in Dynasty*	Construction of Great Wall begins
206 B.C.–A.D. 220	*Han Dynasty*	Contact with Roman Empire
220–589	*Minor dynasties*	Political disunity; invasions
589–618	*Sui Dynasty*	Period of rebuilding
618–907	*T'ang Dynasty*	So-called Golden Age; capital at what is now Sian
907–960	*Minor dynasties*	Period of disorder
960–1279	*Sung Dynasty*	Great age of painting; invention of movable type
1279–1368	*Yuan Dynasty*	Mongol Dynasty founded by Kublai Khan (Marco Polo in China 1274–1292)
1368–1644	*Ming Dynasty*	Last Chinese dynasty
1644–1912	*Ch'ing Dynasty*	Manchu Dynasty (Opium War 1839–42; Taiping Rebellion 1848–65; Boxer Rebellion 1900). Revolution begins in 1911; Chinese Republic proclaimed 1912

Republic of China

1912–	Sun Yat-sen inaugurated provisional president of Chinese Republic
1925–	Death of Sun Yat-sen
1926–28	Nationalists (the Kuomintang), led by Chiang Kai-shek, subjugate warlords, achieve nominal unification of China; capital at Nanking
1931–	Mao Tse-tung proclaims establishment of Chinese Soviet Republic in Kiangsi Province
1932–	Japan completes conquest of Manchuria begun in 1931
1934–36	Under pressure from Chiang Kai-shek's Nationalist troops, Mao Tse-tung and Red Army make the Long March; set up headquarters in Yenan

1937–	Japan begins invasion of China Proper
1945–	Japan's surrender ends World War II; civil war rages between forces of Mao Tse-tung and Chiang Kai-shek
1949–	Communists overrun China (the Liberation); Mao Tse-tung proclaims People's Republic of China; capital at Peking; Nationalists flee to Formosa (Taiwan)

People's Republic of China

1953–	First Five-Year Plan, following collectivization of farms
1954–	Constitution adopted
1957–	Criticism of government temporarily encouraged
1958–	Start of the Great Leap Forward; most industrial objectives fail. Communes established
1960–	China breaks with Soviet Union; Russian technicians sent home
1964–	China explodes its first atomic bomb
1966–69	Cultural Revolution; Red Guards the dominating force
1969–	Clashes with Soviet Union along Manchurian border
1971–	People's Republic of China admitted to UN, replacing Nationalist China
1972–	President Richard M. Nixon visits China
1973–	Diplomatic liaison offices established in Peking and Washington, D.C.

Acknowledgments

No Westerner could hope to have his questions about China today answered without an interpreter of substantial intellectual capacity as well as a facility for understanding the idiom of both the Chinese and English languages. For this I am particularly indebted to Yao Wei, Yu Chung-ching, and Pu Chiao-min.

I express my special appreciation to my colleague, Charles Bennett, whose pictures so well augmented my own for this book. Also a substantial debt is owed to my colleagues from the American Society of Newspaper Editors, whose penetrating and forthright questions developed so much of the information that has gone into these pages.

I am grateful to Catherine Chin, my Chinese teacher, for helping me develop a skill in the language, which not only enriched my journey, but today continues as a new intellectual adventure. To Rose Marie Valco who typed my journal of the trip, typed and re-typed my manuscript; to Mary Ann Nelson and Herbert Hirsch who also assisted; and to my secretary, Bernice Lehmann, go special thanks.

Finally, I must thank Marshall Field, my publisher, for indulging an editor's wanderlust and my wife, Claire, for tolerating those early morning sessions when the only sound in the house was the repetition of Chinese conversation on a tape recorder.

Now, to get ready for the next trip. . . .

EMMETT DEDMON

Index